THE COOL GUIDE

THE COOL GUIDE

Jamie Rix

WALKER BOOKS
AND SUBSIDIARIES
LONDON • BOSTON • SYDNEY • AUCKLAND

First published 2003 by Walker Books Ltd
87 Vauxhall Walk, London SE11 5HJ

2 4 6 8 10 9 7 5 3 1

Text © 2003 Jamie Rix
Illustrations © 2003 Up the Resolution

The right of Jamie Rix and Up the Resolution to be identified as author and illustrator respectively of this work has been asserted by them in accordance with the Copyright, Designs and Patents Act 1988

This book has been typeset in Blockhead, Clarendon, Officina Sans and OptiTypewriter-Special

Printed and bound in Great Britain by
Creative Print and Design (Wales), Ebbw Vale

All rights reserved. No part of this book may be reproduced, transmitted or stored in an information retrieval system in any form or by any means, graphic, electronic or mechanical, including photocopying, taping and recording, without prior written permission from the publisher.

British Library Cataloguing in Publication Data:
a catalogue record for this book is
available from the British Library

ISBN 0-7445-9647-5

www.walkerbooks.co.uk

Preface

OK. Let's start by dragging the facts out into the open.

Boys are cool.
Q.E.D.
The End.

So why do boys so desperately need this self-help book? Well, some boys are cooler than others. Some can pull till the cows come home, while others can't pull a cow. Whichever camp you fall into, this book will change your life. *The Cool Guide* maximizes the potential for cool inside every boy. Even those boys who suffer from that tragic syndrome known simply as The Greater Grunting Spotted Man-Boy Who Knows

What Girls Look Like But Can't Say Hello. Trust us. It is our aim to turn every boy into master of his own tonsils through the easy-to-learn discipline of cool.

Q: So will I get snogged?
A: Yes. That's the whole idea, isn't it?

Being cool is not an end in itself. Boys are only cool for one reason, and that reason is tongue sandwich. So learn these easy-to-follow sixteen and a half steps to heaven and you will be sucking face faster than you can shout "I'm Hannibal Lecter!"

Q: But will I get snogged?
A: You're not listening, are you?

Girls like their boys cool. This is a proven fact. Cool boys are easy – easy to talk to and easy on the eye. *The Cool Guide* is a uniquely scientific programme specially designed to make girls like you. It can be compartmentalized into the following phases:

Phase One:
Admitting You've Got a Problem

Phase Two:
Making the Change
from Fool to Cool

Phase Three:
Taking Your First Cool Steps
into the Big Bad World

Phase Four:
Getting Busy with Lizzie

Phase Five:
Tackling Tongue Sushi

Phase Six:
Cool for Life!

OUR GUARANTEE

If you buy this book and play by its rules, you will become a babe magnet. If you do not buy this book, and choose to ignore its wise teachings, you will find worms in your breakfast cereal every morning for the rest of your life.[1]

If you have any doubt as to the truthfulness of this guarantee, don't take our word for it. Take the word of the world's coolest men. The so-called crew of cool have all read this brilliant book and swear by its incredible pulling powers.[2] Without this book none of them would ever have scored at their first school disco!

THE CREW OF COOL

The Prodigal Son

David Beckham

Wat Tyler

Eminem

Sean Connery

Jonathan Ross

Mahatma Gandhi

Samuel L. Jackson

Johnny Knoxville

Wolfgang Amadeus Mozart

Scooby and Shaggy

Joe Orton

Ian Wright

Robin Hood

The person who invented the air in Nike Air Max trainers

Frank Sinatra

Ned Kelly

Jonny Wilkinson

Nelson Mandela

Bart Simpson

1 This guarantee is nearly as truthful as we can make it on the day of going to print.

2 Probably.

PHASE ONE

ADMITTING YOU'VE GOT A PROBLEM

Step One

Understanding Why You Need Cool

As with all things in life, there is no point in making a change if you don't think that change is necessary. So let's find out if change is required...

Are you tired of beautiful girls rushing past you in the street as if you were nothing more than a pile of steaming dog poo?

❑ **YES** ❑ **NO**

Are you worried that far from strutting your funky stuff to its best effect you don't even know where your funky stuff is?

❑ **YES** ❑ **NO**

When you look into the future do you see a life of lonely nights filled with cold salads and tinned rice pudding, black and white telly, and flea-ridden cats?

❑ **YES** ❑ **NO**

What do you want from your future? An exciting life full of hard-core dancing, thumping bass, fireworks, beach parties and loads of lovely lips?

❑ **YES** ❑ **NO**

If you answer **YES** *to all these questions, boy, do you need our help! CONTINUE...*

So you want to be one of the cool crew. You want to look like a Hollywood superstar, play sport like a Wimbledon champion, be funnier than a joke-shop fart, be cooler than a pair of iced pants and get snogged unconscious at your first party.

Repeat after me: I am a she-magnetizer in the making!

"I am a she-magnetizer in the making!"

Now say grrrrrrrr!

"Grrrrrrrr!"

Now look in the mirror and say it again.

"Grrrrrrrr! Grrrrrrrr! Grrrrrrrr!"

What are you?

"A sheep who'll do anything you tell me?"

Yes! I mean no! You're a tiger!

"I'm a tiger!"

That's better. Well done.

But nobody never got nothing through no work. Getting to the promised land of cool where the rivers flow with sweet sounds and the honeys are thick on the ground is going to be tough. Being cool is not just a face you wear – it requires inner change as well.

Meet Geek.

BEFORE

Geek is the uncoolest boy in the class.

AFTER

This is Geek after a police photofit expert has been let loose with his bag of tricks.

Is "after" Geek cool?

❑ **YES** ❑ **NO**

If you answer **YES***, seek medical advice. Go back to the start immediately and begin your life again. And, this time, pay attention! The answer is obviously* **NO***. "After" Geek is NOT cool. Geek has changed his outward appearance, but inside he's still the same old spotty Herbert he was before. Change must come from within.*

"WELL, I NEVER KNEW THAT!"
FACT FILE #1

Since issuing this "after" picture of Geek, police detectives have arrested Geek for a bank blag in Billericay and a drive-by mooning outside Buckingham Palace.

Throughout this book you will be able to chart Geek's progress towards the Everest of cool and watch as this uniquely scientific programme transforms him from geek to boy cool in sixteen and a half steps.

WHAT GEEK WILL LEARN:

How to be cool

And not a tom fool.

And how to strut funky

And smile like a monkey.

And how to dress bling!

And do his own thing.

And how to put a girl

In a terminal whirl.

If you have come this far, you are now ready to change your life.

READ ON, TIGER...

Step Two

Knowing Who You Are

A doctor doesn't hand out the same pills to each of his patients. Not all Eskimos rub noses with polar bears. And one size of underpants doesn't fit everyone. That's because human beings are not all the same. The same applies to boys. Some boys like goth bands, others think ballroom dancing is a fun way to waste time before they die, and there are even those among them who want to be politicians – these are boys without hope and should be pitied mightily.

Find out who you are by using this in-depth personality profile, specially prepared for *The Cool Guide* by the Institute for the Blindingly Obvious, and Yootwatch, the government focus group charged with understanding youth culture. Their long-awaited report entitled *Lock 'Em Up and Throw Away the Key!* is due for publication shortly.

PERSONALITY TEST

How cool are you right now without even having looked at the utterly brilliant life-changing information contained within this modestly priced work of genius? Try the self-assessment test below:

Test One:

Your mummy tells you to wash your hands for dinner. Do you:

A **Wash your hands for dinner?**
B **Wash your feet for dinner and eat your dinner with your toes?**
C **Tell your mummy to wash her hands, because you are cooking dinner?**

If you answer YES to **A** *you are a mummy's boy and urgently need to cut the cord. Answer YES to* **B** *and you must be a grade A nutter. Answer YES to* **C** *and you are on the right track to Cool Street Station.*

FIRST RULE OF COOL:
There are no rules

Test Two:

You have a six-wire brace fitted. It looks like you've got a Formula One Scalextric track welded to your teeth. Do you:

A **Keep your mouth closed for as long as you've got the brace on, thereby rendering yourself mute?**

B **Stick on a huge bushy moustache to cover your mouth, but otherwise carry on as normal?**

C **Throw a "welcome to my brace" party and invite all of your friends, encouraging them to come along and mock your mouth-scaffolding while enjoying a spectacular display of tooth-wire gymnastics by the chimpanzees from London Zoo?**

Forget the first two. If you answer YES to **C** *please send me an invitation to your next party.*

Test Three:

You have to buy a girl a present. Do you:

A **Buy her a football so she'll give it to you?**

B **Buy her a cake and give it to her with these words: "I just know you're going to love this present. When I first saw you, I thought, Now there's a girl who looks like she really loves her cake!"?**

C **Forget?**

If you answer YES to any of the above you do not know what makes a girl tick. This can only lead to one thing – your face being slapped! Sorry, two things – your face being slapped and your hair being used to wipe clean her plate of spaghetti bolognese. Sorry, three things – your face being slapped, your hair being used to wipe clean her plate of spaghetti bolognese and your favourite football shirt being cut into rags. You are in big trouble, mate.

READ THIS BOOK PRONTO-MONTO!

SECOND RULE OF COOL: Be yourself

Test Four:

You are walking down the street and see a pretty girl approaching you. Do you:

A **Run up to the nearest lamppost and cock your leg?**
B **Sniff a passing dog's bottom?**
C **Bark at lorries?**

If you answer YES to any of the above you are not a boy. **You are a dog.** *Close this book immediately and leave the library.*

Test Five:

You are spending more and more time in your darkened bedroom. Your family suspects that you might be a vampire, you are starting to smell and your best friend is He Who Stares Back From The Mirror.

Do you:

A **Read newspapers and listen to the news on the radio to broaden your understanding of international politics?**

B **Strike one match every hour to burn up your farts?**

C **Grow toadstools in your own discarded earwax, give each toadstool a name and ask them all to be your best friends?**

If you answer YES to **B** *or* **C** *you are a slob. Answer YES to* **A** *and there is a slim chance that you might just turn into an interesting person by mistake.*

THIRD RULE OF COOL:
Girls like boys who have more to say for themselves than "All right?" and "Smashing blouse you've got on!"

Test Six:

You are in a room full of girls. You are trying to impress them. Do you:

A **Remove your trousers and show them two moons rising in Uranus?**

B **Have a "who can pee furthest out of the library window" competition?**

C **Squeeze your spots at them?**

D **Demonstrate the best goal you've ever scored?**

E **Say hello and talk to them?**

If you answer YES to **A**, **B**, **C** *or* **D** *you are a tom fool. Answer YES to* **E** *and you might just stand a rat's whisker of a chance of becoming a cool drool.*

Test Seven:

When you talk to a girl, how would you describe your conversation?

A **What is a conversation?**

If you agree with this answer there is no cure for what you've got. Unfortunately you are a normal boy. Seek help immediately.

You may proceed to the next phase – **Making the Change from Fool to Cool** – only when you have accepted that you have thousands of behavioural defects which need to be corrected. The two most obvious ones are laddishness (including bottom burps and wolf-whistling) and poor conversational skills.

Learn this simple mnemonic. It is WHAT GIRLS WANT. Follow this mnemonic to the letter and you will instantly become sensitive to girls' needs and pay girls the respect that is their due.

T*alk to girls*

I*nterest them with your knowledge*

T*ry to be nice*

S*top acting the giddy goat*

If all boys were this caring, all boys would have girlfriends.

If you have difficulty remembering **T.I.T.S.**, make flashcards to remind yourself and pin the word up in easy-to-view places: on the back of the loo door, on the cover of your English exercise book, on the fridge.

PHASE TWO

MAKING THE CHANGE FROM FOOL TO COOL

Step Three

Think Cool

Now that you have recognized your shortcomings, they can be corrected. Changing what you look like will certainly help to pull the wool over a potential girlfriend's eyes, but if you don't shape up INSIDE as well, you can kiss goodbye to cool fooling.

BE lieve

BE cool

Birds and BE's

It's no good looking cool if inside your head you're still three years old. Asking a girl for a date then taking her to playgroup is NOT going to impress her. So the first thing you must do is make sure you're THINKING cool. To think cool you must think older. To think older grab a pair of specs and read on...

How to Think Yourself into an Older Frame of Mind

1. Become obsessive about making your bed and tidying your room.
2. Look at pictures of yourself as a baby and shake your head in disbelief. Then keep saying "Didn't I look young?" until strangers want to strangle you.
3. Wash the car on Sunday.
4. Eat chocolate. Then say devilishly, "Oh, I know I shouldn't really, but I can't help myself. It's so yummy!"
5. At the supper table, undo the top button of your jeans and release the zip to allow your stomach to hang comfortably like a deflated parachute.
6. Break wind in confined spaces and let everyone know it was you.
7. Discuss mini-roundabouts and their contribution to optimum traffic flow.
8. Fall asleep in front of the telly.

Now that you are thinking older you will discover that you have acquired wisdom and can probably do crosswords and pick the winner in the two forty-five at Haydock Park. But, more importantly, you will not make childish mistakes when you talk to girls.

NOT TALKING GAGA

is fundamental to being cool.

Step Four

New Broom Through Room Cool

Your bedroom and its contents will tell girls who you are. It is therefore vital that your room looks bling! Tidiness, for example, tells girls that you have an analytical or scientific mind, whereas messiness tells them that you have the mind of a small nesting hamster. Having a wooden chair in your bedroom immediately informs girls that you are training to be a lion tamer and will shortly be running away to join the circus. Everything has a story to tell. It's up to you to tell the right story.

WHAT THE OBJECTS IN YOU

poster: You've got a hole in
wall that you made accident
with a friend's head and n
you're trying to hide it.
window: You are a peeping
curtains: You are a vampi
who needs to shut out the l
lamp: Your grandfather was a gecko. You eat moths. This lamp is your frying pan.
alarm clock: During the hours of darkness you mutate into a hibernating hedgehog who finds it hard to wake up.
rug: You are bald.

ROOM TELL A GIRL ABOUT YOU...

teddy bear wallpaper: You still wear nappies.

mirror: You are not a vampire after all.

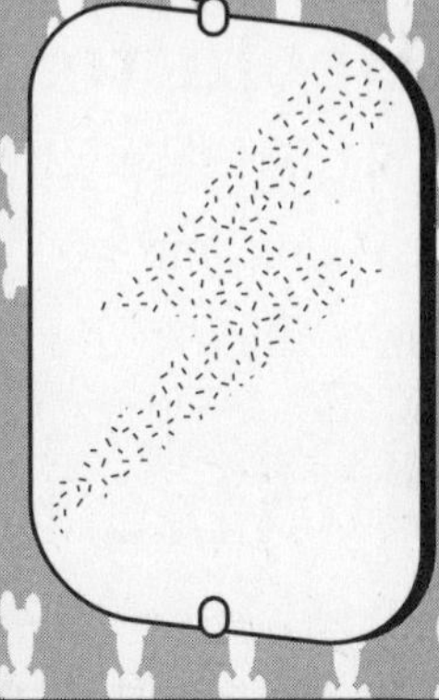

duvet: You are soft and wouldn't last two seconds on the north face of the Eiger. Especially not in pyjamas.

bed: You dream of being an Olympic trampolinist.

goldfish: You haven't got a TV, but you still need something to watch at night. And a circling goldfish is just as interesting.

TV: You are a vegetable.

Take a look at your room. Put yourself in a girl's shoes (having checked for verrucae first, obviously). If a girl was to walk in now, what would she think of you? Does your room say adult cool or baby drool? If the answer is baby drool, you need to make some changes fast.

Decluttering

First, chuck everything babyish away. If there's too much junk and you can't be bothered, simply move room and leave the mess for your parents to sort out.

Moving Room

Clear out the attic, phone up a builder and get a quote for a loft conversion. Ideally you want your own room well away from the prying eyes and wagging ears of your parents. Top of the house is the height of cool. Don't worry about where to put all the junk from the attic. Just dump it in your mum and dad's bedroom. After all, it's *their* mess not yours. And look out for treasure chests. People discover gold and diamonds in their attics all the time. If you get lucky, KEEP the treasure, and resist all attempts by your parents to steal it back. Just because they owned it once does not mean they own it now. If they object and try to blackmail you with emotive phrases like "But my mother gave me that golden tiara just before she died!" or "But that Ming vase was a wedding present!" just say the following words and your parents will shut up and go away: "Finders keepers, losers weepers." Alternatively the following threat can be used: "Touch that vase again, Mama, and you will have an itchy bra."

Both phrases work. With the money you get from selling the treasure, you can forget about the attic conversion and buy your own castle. Owning a castle is even cooler than sharing a Jacuzzi with a Bond girl!

Colours

The coolest colour to paint your room is black. It will match your everyday mood. There are two drawbacks to black that you should consider before buying the paint:

1 It is like living behind a blindfold, therefore you should never leave the window open when you go to sleep. An open window is not visible to the naked eye in the middle of the night. You will fall out while you are trying to take a peeeeeeeeeeeeeeeeeeeeeeeeeeeeeeee.

2 Flies can hide on the walls.

Pink is not a colour I would recommend for a cool room, unless you are the type of boy who regularly drinks gallons of strawberry milkshake until he is sick all over the walls.

Books

Q: Where do we stand on books?
A: In a library when we can't reach the top shelf.

Books on shelves are a good idea, because a boy who is well read will be more interesting than a boy who has only read cereal packets or cheese labels all his life. He may have an in-depth knowledge of what goes into making cheese, but can he discuss the mating cycle of a gadfly? I think not. And it stands to reason that a boy who hasn't studied the mating cycle of the gadfly will not know about **SEX**. And a boy who doesn't know about **SEX** can never be a dad. And a boy who can't be a dad will never get married. And a boy who never gets married will end up living in a rat-infested hovel with scabby dogs instead. So read up about the gadfly or prepare yourself for scabby dogs.

NB: If you haven't got any books, videos-u-like@cheap.com do a nice inexpensive line of fake leatherette video covers which look like books. Nasty! Just put them on your shelves and enjoy the instant thrill of being a clever Trevor. Titles you can choose from include *Harry Potter and the Temple of Doom, Romeo and Jessica Rabbit, Charlie and the Giant Chocolate Orange,* and that great Tolstoy classic, *War and Piccalilli*.

Shelves

If you haven't got any shelves, make some.

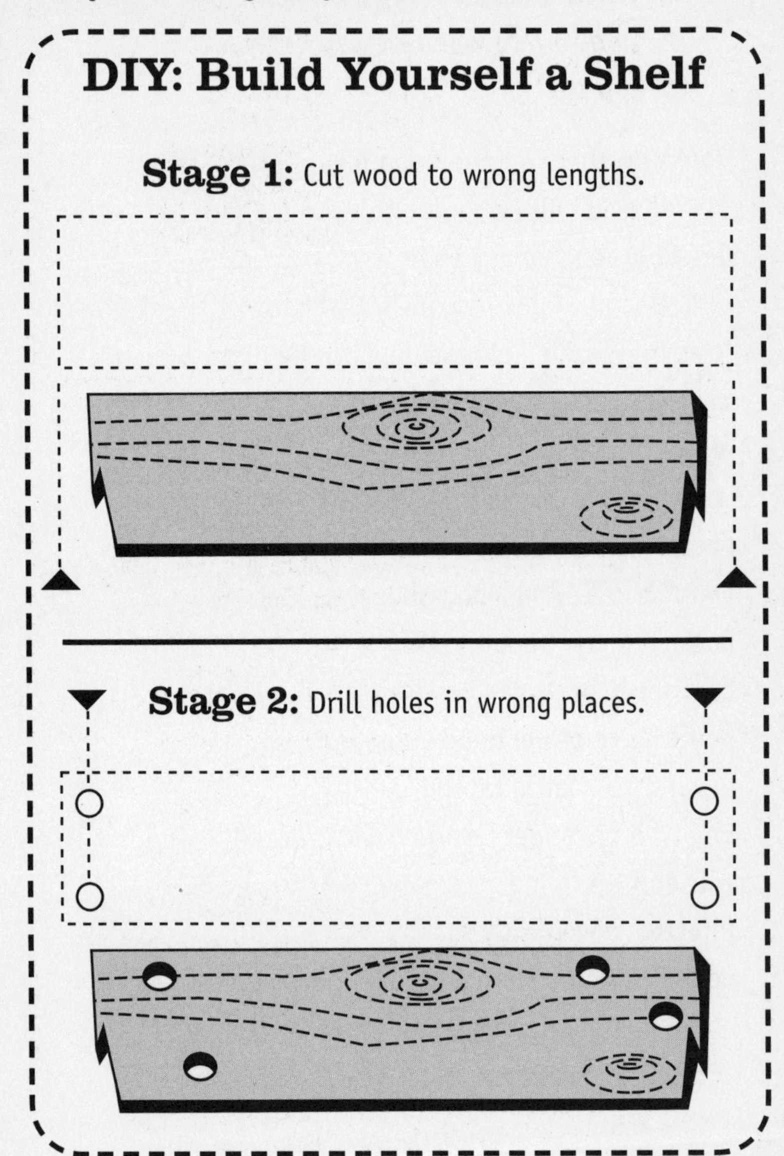

DIY: Build Yourself a Shelf
Stage 1: Cut wood to wrong lengths.
Stage 2: Drill holes in wrong places.

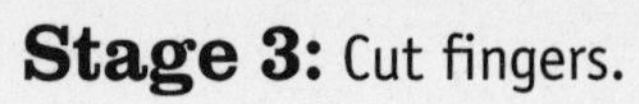

Stage 3: Cut fingers.

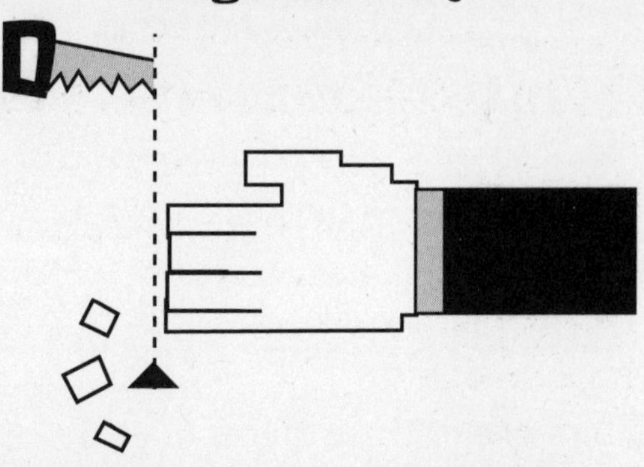

Stage 4:
Lose fingers.

Stage 5:
Have a cup of tea.

Magazines

Magazines are also good to leave lying around. They add an air of sophistication to any room. *Lardy Lads, Leering Lardy Lads* and *Lardy Lads Dropping Their Trousers to Show Their Lardy Bums* are three of the coolest titles that spring to mind.

Sound Systems

Q: Which one of these pieces of equipment should a cool boy have in his bedroom: CD, minidisc, hi-fi, ghetto blaster or gramophone?

A: Yes.

Any self-respecting would-be boy cool, or coolee, must have a sound system. It doesn't matter which one really, so long as it's loud. A loud stereo blocks out the sound of your parents and improves the quality of your life immeasurably. You will notice the following benefits:

1. You will never have chapped hands, because you will never hear your parents screaming at you to come downstairs and help with the washing-up.

2. You will never hear your parents calling you a "@★☼☆ little ☼★@☼-@☆★@ ★★☼@!" when you fail to go and help with the washing-up. Because of this you will not suffer an emotional childhood trauma and will save money on psychiatrist's fees later in life.

3. You will never hear the telephone and the front door bell ring, which means that you will never have to answer them.

4. If you open your window, loud music can make passing girls turn their heads and notice you playing air-guitar in the window. Groovy!

WARNING: *Do not have your sound system so loud that your ears bleed, because getting plasters to stick to your eardrums is a painful business. It's a bit like posting your love spuds through a spring-loaded letter box, only worse.*

Doors

Door signs are very important for creating an aura of cool. Not only are they hysterically funny, they can be quite moving too, like this one:

Quite a lot of door signs have connections to farts, but that's cool, because cool boys are great fart lovers.

FOURTH RULE OF COOL:
Fart first, laugh later

DO NOT ENTER –
THIS IS FART HELL
CALL A DOCTOR,
I'M HAVING A FART ATTACK

THIS ROOM BELONGS
TO CABBAGE FUMES

TOOT!
IF YOU HAD BEANS LAST NIGHT

Then there are the classics:

XXX DANGER XXX
LOVE BEAST ON THE LOOSE

HAREM
PLEASE WIPE YOUR BOOTS

GENIUS AT WORK
in the next room ☛

Any door sign is good,
but the best by far is:

because girls will walk into your bedroom and undress!

Walls

Finally, what should a boy cool have on his bedroom walls?

Not bogeys: Girls are not impressed that you can flick a bogey two metres up your wall. They are even less impressed that you've left the offending green one ON the wall for everyone to see. "I'm proud of it!" is not an excuse. Nor is "But it's a world-record snot put!"

Posters: You must select your posters very carefully.

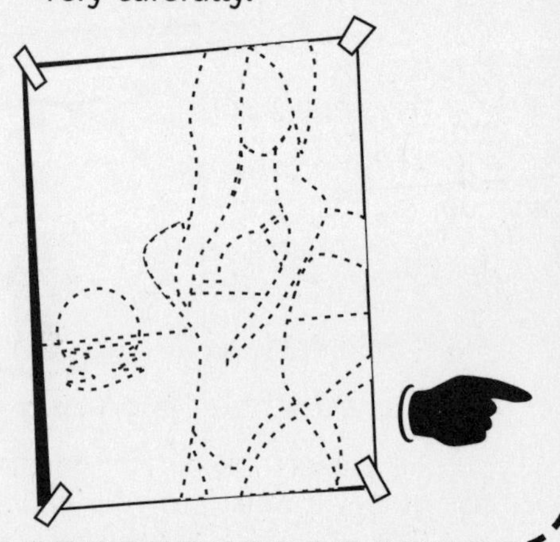

POSTERS THAT ARE OUT

- ☒ kittens with bows
- ☒ puppies sleeping inside slippers
- ☒ monkeys wearing your granddad's clothes and drinking tea
- ☒ boy bands wearing white pirate shirts slashed to the waist
- ☒ showjumping
- ☒ flowers
- ☒ football (girls don't like football)

POSTERS THAT ARE IN

- ☑ famous gangster films
- ☑ kung fu masters
- ☑ racing cars
- ☑ deadly snakes and insects
- ☑ adult cartoons
- ☑ bad-boy bands
- ☑ girls in bikinis

Q: What if my mum won't allow me to have a half-naked lady on my bedroom wall?

A: Sometimes your mum won't allow you to have a half-naked lady on your bedroom wall. If so, this is what you must do...

The Half-Naked Lady Scam

With a chisel and hacksaw cut a secret panel into the wall behind the offending half-naked lady poster. Then hang this panel on two ball and socket pivot hinges and attach a length of rope to the panel. The rope should run through a simple pulley mechanism attached to the wall and be tied to the handle of the bedroom door. Then, each time the bedroom door opens, the rope tightens and the secret panel spins on its axis, thereby hiding the offending half-naked lady poster from the person entering the room. When the door is shut again the poster spins back, to the obvious delight of everyone left in the room.

If, however, your mother is cunning and knows a thing or two about secret panels and pulley mechanisms, you might find that instead of opening the door and leaving it open, she steps into the room and CLOSES THE DOOR BEHIND HER. This means, of course, that the secret panel will spin back revealing the half-naked lady poster while your mother is still in the room, and your ingenious attempt to hide the half-naked lady will have failed. There is a solution, but you will need two dozen empty egg boxes to break your mother's fall.

Cut a further secret panel in the floorboards just in front of the door. Attach another rope to this floor panel, pass it through another highly secret pulley and tie it to the door handle next to the first rope. Now, when your mother stands in your bedroom and shuts the door, the second pulley mechanism will open the floor trap and she will plummet through the ceiling into the sitting room below, where you have stacked the empty egg boxes to cushion her landing.

Q: What if my mother spots the ropes before she closes the door? Won't she smell a rat?

A: Not if you wind paper chains and tinsel around the ropes and disguise them as Christmas decorations.

Q: Why didn't I think of that?

A: Because I'm a book and you are stupid.

Follow the nits over the page to find out what you need to change next!

Step Five

Looking After the Flowers in the Temple of Cool

The temple in question is your body. You are your own church. You must fill your own pews, arrange the flowers in your own nave, and trim the candles in your own rectory. In other words, pamper your body in the right way and you will look cool. Let it go and you will look and smell like a sack of steaming horse manure – not cool at all! Let's start at the top...

Hair

Hair is everything. What you do with your hair says more about you than those signs that medieval villains used to wear round their necks on their way to the gallows or stocks. Signs like THIEF and PIG STEALER and COMPUTER HACKER.

Hair comes in many different styles:

Skinhead or Number One: Obviously this cut is low maintenance, but you've got to have a good-shaped head to carry it off. Most boys have creased heads like walnuts, oval heads like creatures from outer space or flat heads like Table Mountain. Boys with scary heads like these should never go nearly bald. They will frighten pets and give old people heart attacks.

"WELL, I NEVER KNEW THAT!" FACT FILE #2

Most girls like something floppy at the front for them to run their fingers through.

Mullet: This is high on top, short at the sides and long at the back, and is a hideous haircut only worn by people with spotty necks who want to hide their bleepers from public view. Do not have a mullet or people will make fun of your spotty neck whether you have one or not. You will end up with nicknames like the Scarlet Pimple or Spot the Dog or Pus the Bucket, Old Man, I'm Going to Be Sick!

Periwig: A periwig is not a wig worn by the famous teenager Perry. It is a white wig that makes you look like a judge or a lady, depending on how tall it is. It looks like you've got a crouching poodle on your head. Wigs can sometimes be very useful if you have snogged an ugly girl by mistake while the lights were off at a disco and now she wants to go out with you. You can put the periwig on and stroll around town with complete confidence that she will never recognize you.

WARNING: *Check that the ugly girl is not a fan of crouching poodles first or she may approach the periwig to feed it a dog biscuit and find you crouching underneath.*

Perm: These are tight curls that make you look like your granny. A perm also makes you look like you are wearing grapes on your head. This style is to be avoided, unless you want alcoholic people treading on your hair in a desperate attempt to squish themselves a glass of wine.

Ponytail: Oh dear! This is a girl's hairstyle! No, no, no, no, NO! It is not cool. The only boys who are allowed to wear ponytails are old rock stars or old goalkeepers, and society only tolerates them because they won't be alive for much longer. If you have a ponytail you have a choice. Either cut it off or buy a dress.

Lardy Locks: This is shoulder-length hair which has not been cut or washed for six months. It hangs like limp rat's tails dipped in lard. If you can imagine brushing your hair every day with a comb made from pork pies, lardy locks would be the result. Except that lardy locks are NEVER brushed. There's not a comb in the world that can break through these tangles. It is not surprising that girls hate lardy locks, even though they do have some uses. For example, swimming the English Channel. If you have forgotten your all-over body grease, simply scrape down the lardy locks and use the sebaceous excretions instead of blubber! But beware of Japanese whaling ships when you're in the water; they might mistake you for a humpback whale.

Mohican: Don't touch it with a totem pole. You will be expelled from school. And who wants a haircut that looks like the barber fell asleep before he finished?

Waxed Hair: Cool, unless you work in a candle factory.

Dreadlocks: Cool. Nuff said.

Spots

Q: Why am I the only person on the planet to have spots?

A: You're not.

Q: But I never see anyone else with spots.

A: Yes, you do. They're just better at covering them up.

Q: What about royalty? Royal children never have spots.

A: That's because they've got servants to have their spots for them.

Q: You mean there are servants who grow royal children's spots on their own faces?

A: That's right. Royalty have servants to do all those unpleasant little jobs that we mere mortals have to put up with.

Q: Such as?

A: Being sick, going to the loo and having our nipples pierced.

Q: Well, I never.

A: And neither do they.

Are you frit of a zit? When you're cool you won't give a second thought to your spots, because cool boys drive on CHARISMA, which neutralizes all known bleepers. But for those of you would-be boy cools who desperately want to be cool about spots but still need help, here are a few tricks of the trade to help you overcome your fear of the zitmeister!

The Full-Face Cover-Up: The most effective way to cover a spot is a woollen balaclava, but woollen balaclavas are not very practical in hot weather and cause facial sweating, which in turn causes more spots than the balaclavas are covering up. You need something that provides an all-over cover while at the same time allowing air to circulate around your face so that your spots can heal. You need a material that lets your bleepers breathe. And what better material than skin? A severed goat's head is an effective cover-up, or fish skin wrapped tightly round the face like a badly tied turban. If neither is available, a simple wicker shopping basket will do.

Face-Painting: Face-painting is a novel way to turn a big throbbing spot on your face into something amusing with which to entertain your friends. Make you and your spot the talking point of the party with creative face-painting. Turn a yellow pus volcano into a highly comical fried egg! Simply paint around the spot and create whatever object comes to mind: a Mexican sombrero, a scaled-down model of Saturn and its rings, or how about my favourite – you'll need a double header for this one, but it's worth it – Madonna's famous bra!

The Big Squeeze: "To squeeze, or not to squeeze: that is the question." And this is the answer – **BEWARE!** Squeezing spots is fraught with danger for the would-be lover. Imagine this… You're going out to meet a girl. As you leave the house you notice a tiny red splodge on your chin. It seems so simple. One quick squeeze and bye-bye, ugly spot; hello, perfect loveliness! The reality is very different. Tragically, many dates are lost through post-squeezematic stress (PSS), when those tiny red splodges turn out to be pusbergs with more than seven-eighths of their evil mass lurking beneath the skin. What you planned as a quick spurt turns into a major archaeological dig. And when you've finished, that tiny red splodge has been transformed into a huge hole in the middle of your face half as wide as the Grand Canyon and three times as deep.

Q: So is it cool to squeeze spots?

A: No.

Shaving

A boy's first shave is a personal Holy Grail. Nothing is quite as important to a boy as scraping a strip of cold steel across a hairless nest of spots on his top lip, and watching his face burst into several bubbling streams of frothy red blood. The eminent Chinese philosopher Confucius, he say: "If we reach our dreams we are dead. That is why it is every boy's dream to start shaving and every man's dream to stop." Confucius, he knew a thing or two about shaving. He had a beard. Cool boys wait until they've got hair on their face before starting to shave.

If you don't know whether you should be shaving yet or not, use our fabulous bumfluffometer to help you decide.

Bumfluffometer
1 mm
Call that bumfluff? You're still a baby! No shave.
2 mm
It's fluffier and bummier, but still no shave.
3 mm
Sharpen that razor. You're nearly a man.
5 mm
Shave! Shave! Shave!
10 mm
Seek advice from a zoo.

YOU THINK YOU'VE GOT PROBLEMS?

Body Hair – The Big Debate!

Hairy Mary is an agony aunt. She answers your questions on the burning issues of the day.

QUESTION OF THE WEEK
Do girls find hairy boys more or less attractive?

HAIRY MARY WRITES:

Hello and welcome to **Body Hair – The Big Debate.** We have two boys to debate this question, Cain and Abel. One is an hairy boy; the other is totally smooth.

THE HAIRY BOY WRITES:
Girls find body hair very sexy. Even on toes. It's a monkey thing. Human ancestors would comb through each other's hair looking for lice and fleas. That's what they called entertainment. Today we've got *Blind Date*, but girls still like a good lice and flea hunt now and then. If you haven't got any body hair of your own, rip it out of your dad's chest while he's asleep. Then stick it under your arms with the yolk of a whisked egg. But hurry before he wakes up and asks for it back.

THE SMOOTH BOY WRITES:
Girls have got soft skin, so beards feel like rough sandpaper to them. If you do a lot of kissing there is a real possibility that you might sand her away altogether. Also, have you ever heard a girl say that her favourite animal is a grizzly bear or an orangutan? Of course not. Girls like smooth animals such as seals and dolphins and fish, which just goes to prove that I must be right. Slippery – that's what girls want their boyfriends to be. Chuck me that beach ball. On my head…

HAIRY MARY WRITES:
Let's ask a girl…

A GIRL WRITES:
I don't care if he's hairy or not, so long as he likes puppies.

HAIRY MARY WRITES:
So there we have it. Next week it's body piercing. We meet the woman with seven thousand piercings on her body and ask her why she's called **THE HUMAN COLANDER.**

WRITE Send your problems to HAIRY MARY (unless they are boils. Boils tend to burst in the post).

So you're looking good. You've got the hairstyle of your choice, you've painted your spots and you've had a shave (or not, depending on the results from the bumfluffometer).

YOUR BODY IS READY TO COOL OUT WITH GIRLS!

Or is it?

Ever heard of  ?

Hope on a Rope

Soap is something that boys do not like to get too close to. Unfortunately a boy who doesn't use soap is something that *girls* do not like to get too close to. A boy stinking like something that has just been recovered from a pig's toilet into which a farmer has scraped a bucket of thickly oozing toe jam is not a girl's idea of heaven. So here's a thought. It's cool to wash.

And here's a tip for those of you who are physically repulsed by the mere thought of water touching your skin. Ask Granny to give you some seriously pongy aftershave for Christmas, then splash it all over.

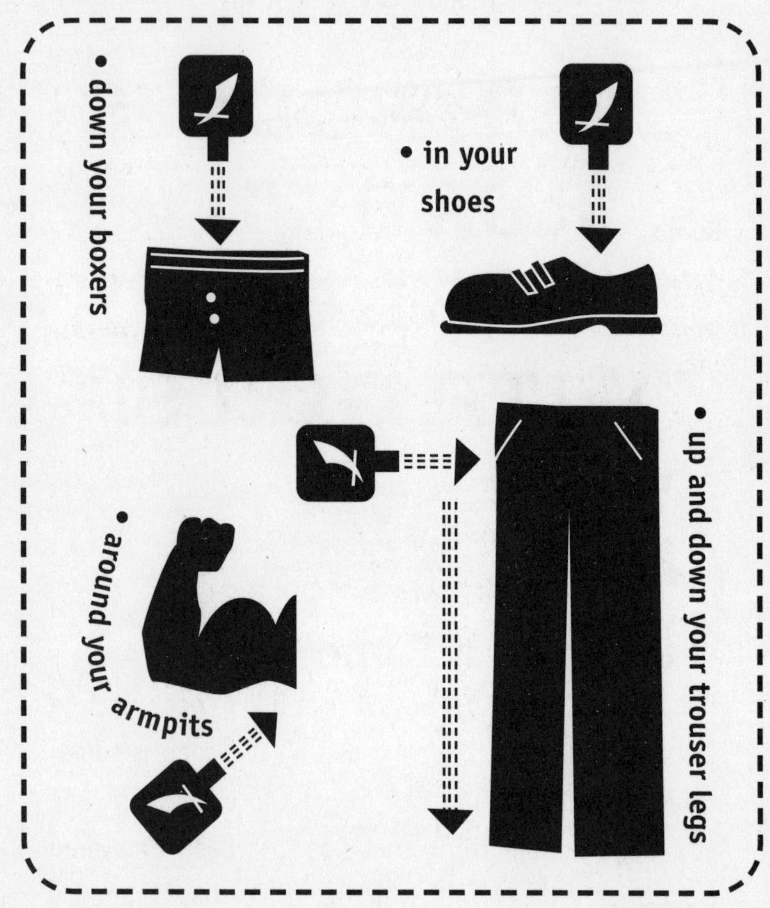

• down your boxers
• in your shoes
• up and down your trouser legs
• around your armpits

You'll be glad that you did ... until the stinging kicks in, that is!

Step Six

Dress Cool

By now you should be smelling gorgeous, looking gorgeous and the proud possessor of such gorgeously waxed hair that it resolutely refuses to move, even in a force nine gale. That's the hanger dealt with. Now you've got to hang something on it.

Q: What's the point of it all?

A: The point of wearing cool clothes is to attract the girls. It is the same throughout the animal kingdom. The peacock struts his flashy fantail when he fancies taking a peahen home for a quick peck. The warthog squirts his fruity fart juice when he fancies a roll in the mud with his piggy missus. It's all about display. And so it is with boys.

FIFTH RULE OF COOL:
Don't be a sheep

Have you ever wondered why sheep don't have names? It's because you cannot tell them apart. They all look the same.

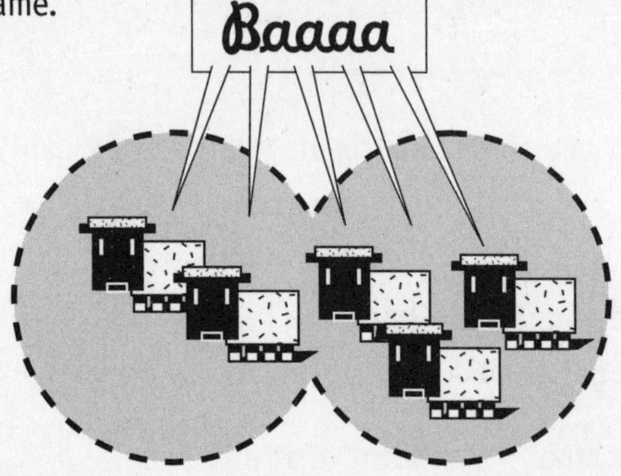

Now take a look in the playground. Do you see the similarity?

It is a myth that you show off your individuality by dressing like everyone else. And lest you forget – sheep always come to a sticky end.

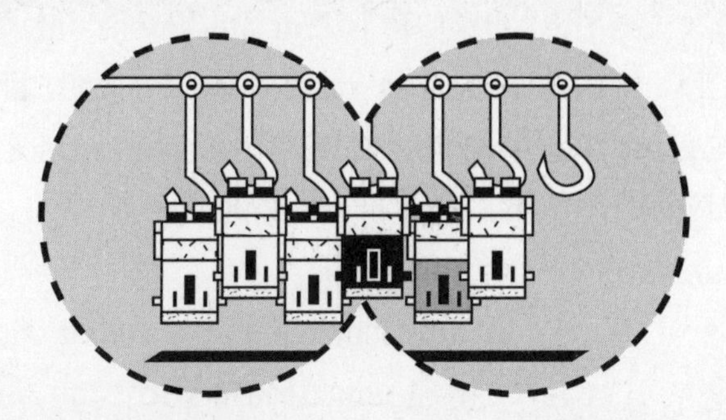

So don't just go for the fashionable labels that everyone else is wearing. Be different. Look elsewhere.

Be Different: Cool clothes are ones that are DIFFERENT from everyone else's. Why would you want to look the same? You're not in the army. So choose clothes with individual flair. A hat, a string vest, a Hawaiian shirt, ski goggles, Bermuda shorts!

Hysterical Historical: If you don't have any ideas of your own for a cool costume, why not take a look back through history and steal ideas from the past? Be a fop or a dandy. Amuse the girls with your pantaloons and tights. Intrigue them with the lure of your codpiece. And have them beating a path to your door to try on your frock coat.

Baggy: If you're stuck for different ideas, then here's a tip that will see you right no matter what the social occasion. **BAGGY IS COOL**. In fact, the baggier your clothes the better. It is crucially important that NOTHING fits you. Clothes must hang off your body like rags off the Incredible Hulk. Trousers must not sit any higher than the back of the knees so that ALL of your underpants can be seen.

The ultimate cool in casual baggy is called showing skin. That is wearing your trousers so baggy that they lie scrunched round your ankles. Combine this sitting-on-the-loo look with baggy underpants and you can easily achieve showing skin. Your naked bum cheeks will be wobbling in full view. Chilly!

Accessories: Baggy jewellery is also cool. Great big chunks of gold like slabs of chocolate, so heavy that you'll break your wrist if you wave too suddenly. Baggy gold chains round your neck like industrial bicycle locks, and gold on your fingers – bulky, round rings like bird baths, big enough for a family of six to splash about in. However, jewellery is very expensive, so here's a make-over tip.

THE JEWELLERY
MAKE-OVER KIT

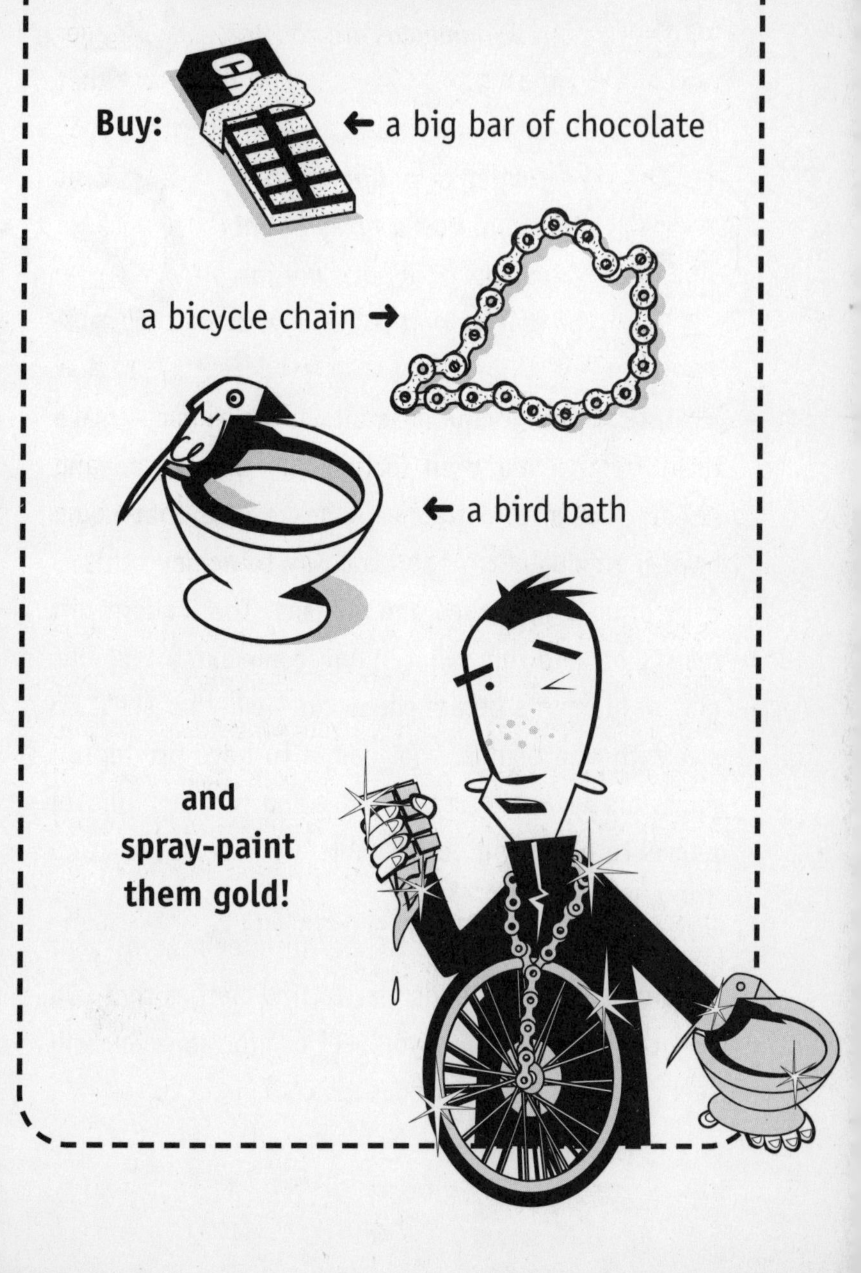
Buy:
a big bar of chocolate
a bicycle chain
a bird bath
and
spray-paint
them gold!

Rucksacks are sweet ...
but handbags are dodgy.

A pet is for life, not for wearing as a funky hat at a cool party, and not for leaving on the bus either.

Pants: Never compromise on pants. Pants can make the difference between feeling like a love god and feeling like an old tramp. So make sure that yours have individual flair. The best way to achieve this is with printed messages and slogans. The modern girl insists on knowing what funny comment a boy has got on his pants before she decides whether she'll go out with him or not. Cool names to have printed on pants are MR MUSCLE, PANTS OF FIRE and THE ROCK. Uncool names to have printed on pants are MADE IN CHINA and 100% NYLON.

As well as aiming to be different with your wardrobe, you should also try to find clothes that you feel comfortable in. If you feel comfortable you will feel confident, and confident is cool.

Be Comfortable: Have you thought of rummaging through your dad's old clothes? No. Actually, NO! There is a limit. You don't want to look like your dad, however much he might want to look like you because it makes him feel younger. And don't wear your mum's old clothes either, because high heels and dresses look better on girls.

Your big brother's hand-me-downs are all right, so long as they don't come at a price. If your big brother says, "You can only have my hand-me-downs if you give me one hundred pounds in cash and all your computer games!" then don't take them. He is simply trying to enslave you like all big brothers do, and when he has got you in his power he will work you to the bone doing all those nasty jobs that he doesn't want to do for himself (for example cleaning dog muck off his trainers and phoning up his long-term girlfriend and telling her she's dumped).

Granny's hand-knitted cardigans, the ones that she gives you every Christmas, often make surprisingly useful additions to your wardrobe. Of course, they're big and stretch to infinity and beyond, and the one she knitted you last Christmas would make a smashing waistcoat for an elephant, but think again! Don't just see this knitted object as a cardigan. Imagine it as an overcoat or, better still, a dual-purpose overcoat and sleeping bag! How cool would that be, to turn up at a party wearing your own bed! Or – and this could make you rich and famous – it could be a tea cosy for the biggest teapot in the world out of which you could drink one hundred cups of tea in four minutes and twenty-four seconds, thereby becoming the Guinness world-record holder! Or you could rent it out as a cargo net to the British Army for transporting jeeps under helicopters. Or, if you ever needed to jump out of a window and run away from home, you could always use your granny's cardigan as a parachute!

One item of clothing is unique. Whatever else you wear, do NOT leave home without your trainers. Trainers are cool because they're different and comfortable.

Trainers: Trainers maketh the boy. Trouble is, trainers also maketh the boy broketh, because they cost so much. However, it is a fact that the coolest trainers are the most expensive. This government chart produced by the Ministry of Cool proves the link between coolness and cost:

☛

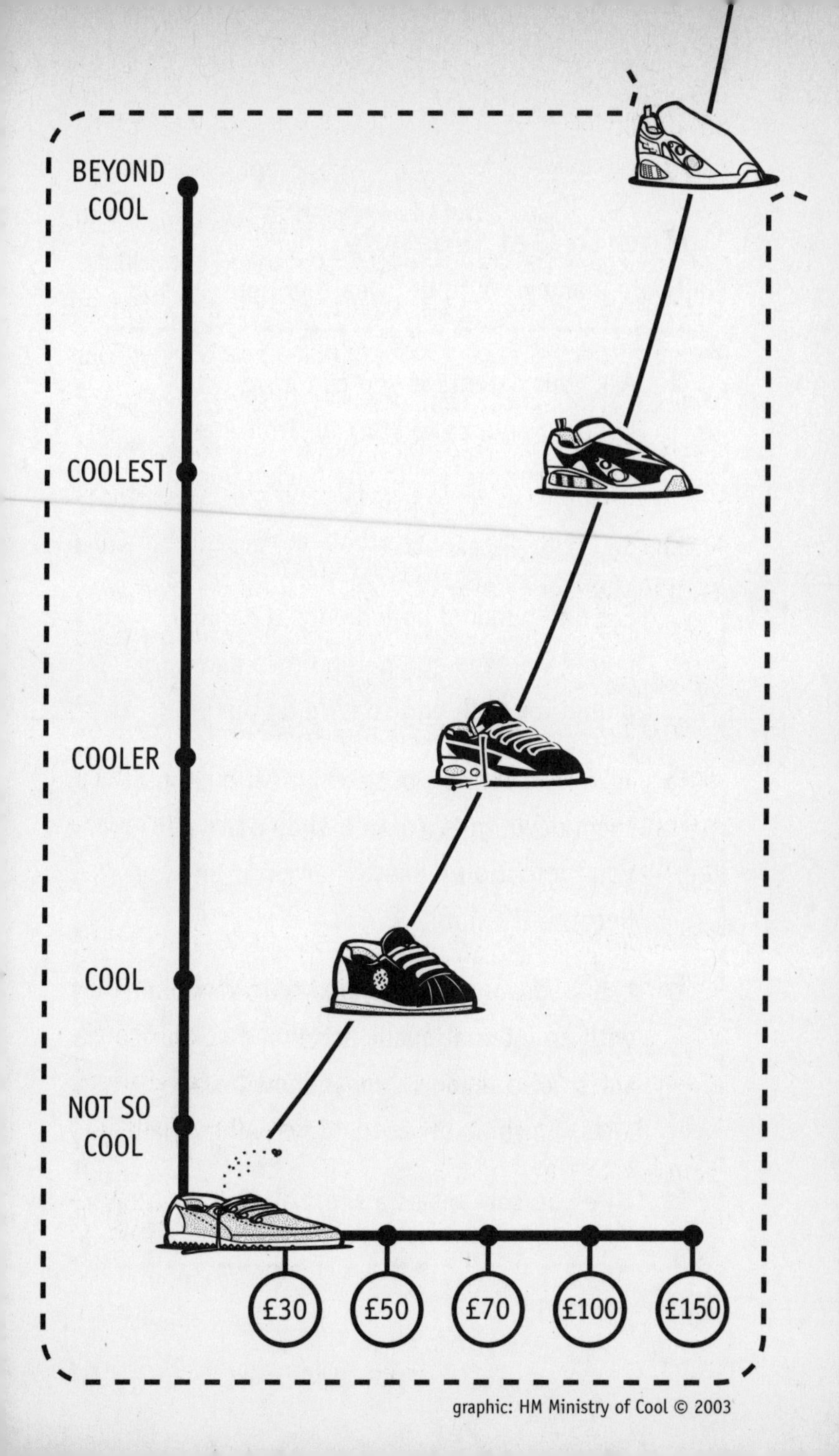
BEYOND
COOL
COOLEST
COOLER
COOL
NOT SO
COOL
£30
£50
£70
£100
£150
graphic: HM Ministry of Cool © 2003

So if you want to be the coolest cat at the party you've got to get wealthy.

How to Get Wealthy

There are many ways to get wealthy. Here are six:

1. Ask your parents if you can have two hundred pounds to start an Iron Age settlement project in the back garden.
2. Sell your sister.
3. Eat one hundred boiled eggs. Charge a pound for each egg going down and a pound for each egg coming up again.
4. Take worms to school and threaten to put them down girls' socks if they don't pay you protection money. Then do it anyway, because it's funny.
5. Learn shadow puppetry and tour the country with an internationally acclaimed box office smash of a shadow puppet show for all ages, finishing off at the Royal Albert Hall.
6. Hire yourself out as a short alien.

Q: What if none of these suggestions work and I don't have any money?

A: In an emergency you only need one item of clothing. You can wear any old clothes and STILL keep your cool as long as you wear this accessory.

Q: Why?

A: It has the power of cool built in.

Q: Boxer shorts?

A: Get outta here, man! Shades.

Shades: Without changing anything about yourself, shades turn you from a geek into an international man of mystery, and girls love a bit of mystery in a man! How else do you explain the appeal of Gary Barlow? The mystery is why he was ever famous in the first place.

It is also no coincidence that "shades" is spelled HADES with an S on the front. They are wicked and bring out the devil in a man.

→ If you walk into a party looking like a geek you will get fruit punch over your head.

→ If you walk into a party looking like a preppy you will get chocolate gateau over your trousers.

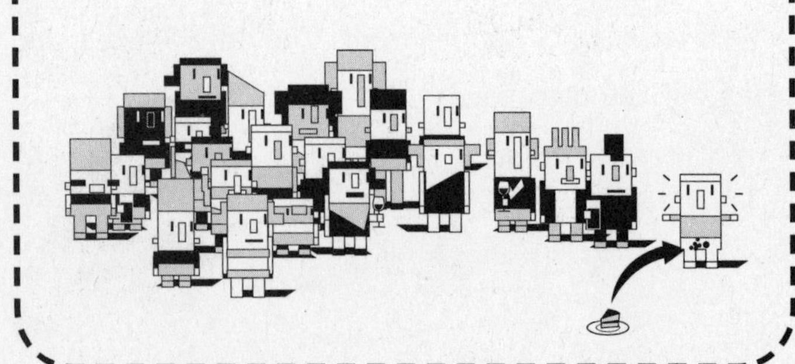

➜ If you walk into a party wearing shades you will get girls all over you!

➜ And maybe a broken shin or two. A cracked skull, a few broken toes, a bruised hip and a dislocated knee. In the darkened atmosphere of a party, shades can sometimes make seeing rather tricky.

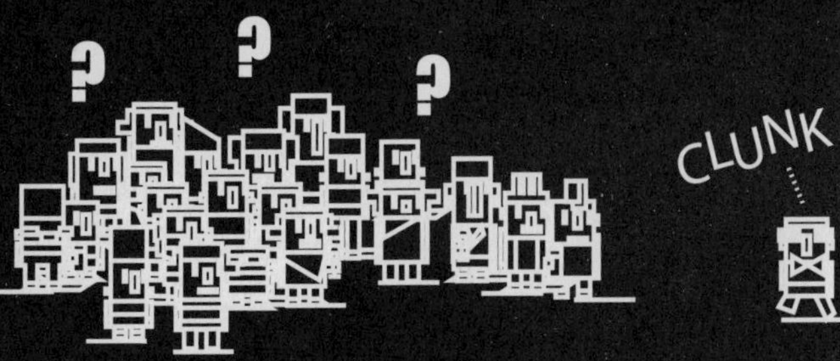

Despite the obvious dangers, shades are still the best, cheapest and quickest way to look cool, whether worn:

up on the top of the head,

backwards on the back of the head,

or hanging loosely round the throat.

Shades may also be worn across the bridge of the nose as a sort of visor in front of the eyes, but only if you want to look like a sad has-been. Bridge-shades are tragic and just *so* yesterday.

Step Seven

School Cool – U and Non-U Uniforms

Q: You keep telling me to dress differently from other boys if I want to look cool.

A: And your point is?

Q: What do I do at school when all boys have to wear the same uniform?

A: I'm going to ask you a question. Why do boys go to school?

Q: To study maths and English and pass exams?

A: Oh yes, that's what they want you to believe. A boy goes to school to study girls and pass love notes.

Q: And your point is?

A: If a boy goes to school to study girls, he must apply the same rule of cool to his uniform as he applies to all his other clothes.

Q: But it's a uniform! It's the same as everyone else's. How can one uniform be different from another?

A: Tiny little changes. Infinitesimal gestures of defiance. Anything to catch the lady's eye!

Q: I see. Like a strutting peacock or a farting warthog.

A: Now you've got it!

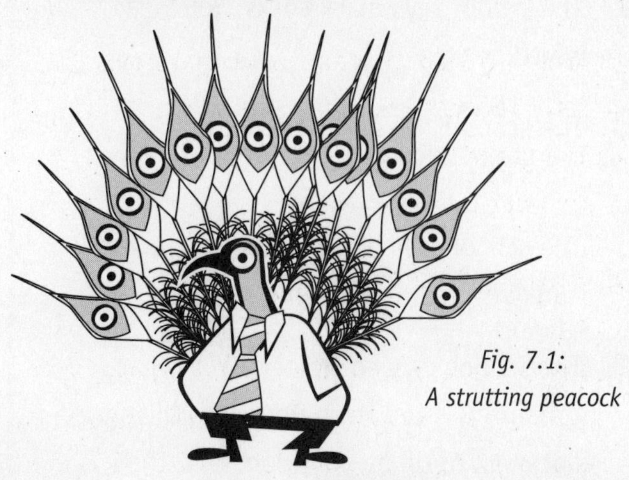

Fig. 7.1: A strutting peacock

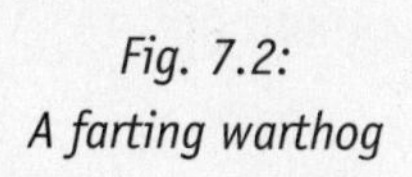

Fig. 7.2: A farting warthog

Q: So how do I make these tiny little changes to my school uniform?

A: Know the school rules...

THE SCHOOL RULES

1. The school says black socks. You wear white.

2. The school says shirts tucked in. You untuck.

3. The school says black jumpers. You wear blue with red and green stripes.

4. The school says no trainers. You wear trainers and tell them your sensible shoes got chewed up by your dog, who then sadly died and was cremated at the pet crematorium with your shoes still inside it.

5. The school says black coats only. You wear blue denim and tell them you're colour-blind.

6. The school says top buttons done up. You undo, and tell them you need the extra space for your Adam's apple, which you're expecting to appear any day now when your voice breaks.

7 The school says ties should be regulation length. You knot yours in a tortoise. A tortoise tie has a huge fat knot like a tortoise's body, and a teeny-weeny tie poking out of the bottom, just like a tortoise's tail.

8 The school says smart. You rip your blazer pockets. When the headteacher asks you why your pockets are flapping like a boxer dog's ears, you say, "Pocket billiards, miss. I was playing pocket billiards and my cue slipped!" You will probably get a detention, but you will also get admiring looks from loads of girls who think you're wickedly brave!

**SIXTH RULE OF COOL:
Cool at school means break the rule**

THE PATENTED "PLAN YOUR OWN OUTFIT" PLANNER

Cut-Out Ken is scientifically designed to help you choose a different look from your friends. Once you have chosen your own unique look, you may MOVE ON...

Step Eight
Shop Cool

When a boy steps up to the oche of life to throw his first dart into the dartboard of manhood, he makes a choice. Cool or fool? You have been brave and chosen the path of cool. Like many other would-be coolees who have followed this path before you (for example Elvis Presley, Michael Owen, Robbie Williams), you must now face the reality of what you have done.

Now that you have chosen a unique look for yourself, you must face the problem that brings in its wake more stress than any human being should ever have to cope with in one lifetime. It's called shopping.

Oh yes, it sounds innocent enough, doesn't it? But shopping involves leaving the house. Shopping involves walking down the street. Shopping involves MEETING OTHER PEOPLE! Now do you see the problem? No? Right...

Q: If the only way to be cool is to wear cool gear, and the only way to wear cool gear is to go out and buy it, how can I buy cool gear in public BEFORE I'm wearing cool gear? Won't people take one look at my old clothes and think I'm uncool?

A: Yes. This is called the shopping conundrum. My advice to you is only go out after dark.

Q: But people will think I'm a vampire.

A: People have thought that of teenage boys for centuries. Pay no attention, unless friends and family members start creeping into your bedroom at night with a mallet and a stake. Only then will you need to explain yourself.

A simple alternative to only going out after dark is to wear a large paper bag over your head. Make sure it covers you down to your ankles. With the bag in place you can safely shop for cool gear in broad daylight and nobody will see your uncool clothes underneath. Avoid large dustbins as passers-by will tend to scrumple you up and throw you away.

If you cannot find a large enough paper bag, an unobtrusive pantomime horse costume will do just as well.

Q: It's all very well telling me to disguise myself, but I'm not allowed to shop on my own. I don't buy my own clothes.

A: That's not a question.

Q: Sorry. How do I deal with She With Her Hands On The Purse Strings? She of no taste, who hates what I like. She who buys my clothes BIG for comfort and long-wearing practicality!

A: You mean your mother! There's nothing you can do about her. Mothers have taken their sons shopping since fashion stores first started in Roman times. So get used to it.

"WELL, I NEVER KNEW THAT!"

FACT FILE #3

It's true! Thousands of years ago Roman boys were being embarrassed by their mothers in stores such as Nextus, Gapicus, Benettonicus and Gallic Connection.

So how can you deal with your mother?

Pretending Your Mother Isn't There:

There are precautions you can take to minimize the embarrassment of being seen shopping with the she-devil. The key is pretending you're not with her:

1. When being driven into town, lie on the back seat of the car so that no one can see you. If they can't see you they won't know you're there. If she asks what you're doing, tell her you've just been carsick and are licking the lumps off the carpet. She will not ask again!

2. When you get out of the car, pretend you've seen something in a shop window and make a beeline for it, ignoring your mother's cries of "Wait for me, darling!"

3. When you enter a shop, never enter together. Be polite. Open the door for her, then pretend to get stuck holding the door open for the next three hundred customers. In this way you can allow your mother to get thirty-six metres ahead of you, so that you enter the store alone.[3]

3 Government statistics show that thirty-six metres is the correct distance to be separated from your mother in a department store. Any less and she will insist on controlling you like a dog.

Keeping a Safe Distance from Your Mother: When out shopping in public there are certain safe distances that should always be observed between mother and son. These distances have been scientifically calculated by the Department of Embarrassment so that boys know exactly how far they must hang back from their mothers before girls think they're grown-ups out shopping on their own.

Observing the statutory safe distance from his mother ensures that the boy will always have sufficient time to run and hide should his mother unexpectedly turn and call out his name.

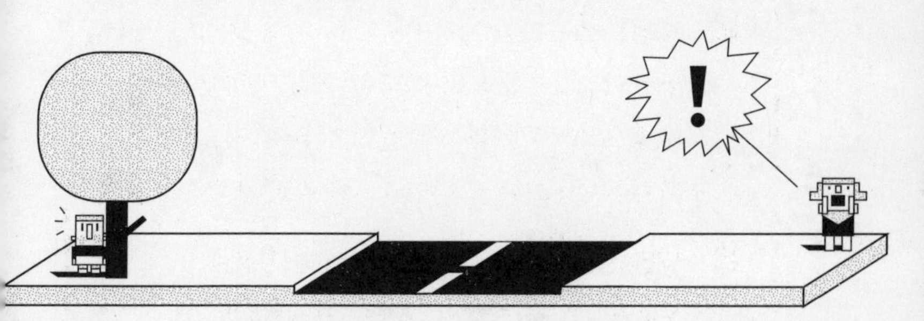

Open space = 73 metres

See overleaf for a fully comprehensive chart of Safe Separation Distances from Mother.

SAFE SEPARATION DISTANCES FROM MOTHER

Crowded space = 6 metres. Plenty of people to hide behind.

Busy street = 23 metres. Shop windows provide ideal hiding places.

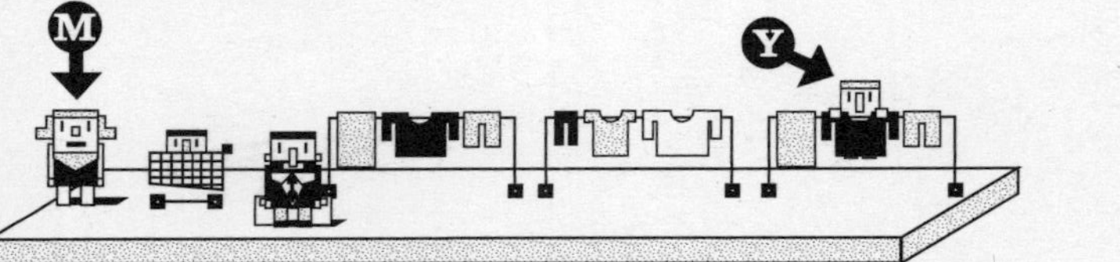

Large store = 36 metres. Hiding in racks of clothes is not always practical.

LEGEND

M Mother

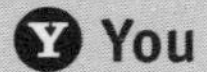 You

NB: Of course, these distances should be doubled if it is raining, as slippage will add extra seconds to any manoeuvre.

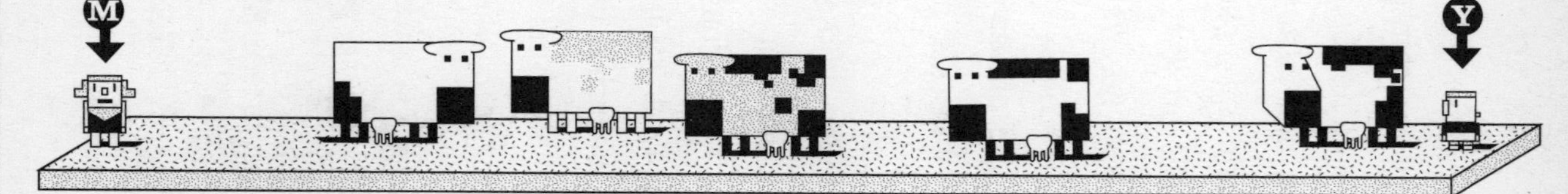

Quiet street = 53 metres. You'll need time to hide unless you're good at impersonating postboxes.

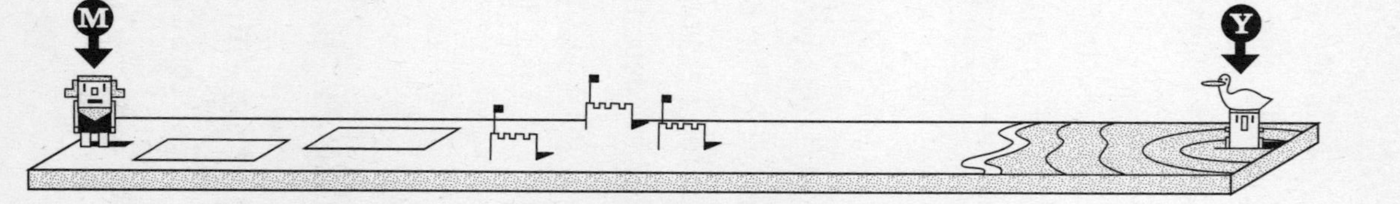

Open space (park or beach) = 73 metres. Brush up your duck calls.

Countryside = 96 metres. Learn to milk a cow.

Refuse to Be Your Mother's Dolly: When you're trying on clothes, your mother will tug at you and spin you round to inspect the clothes from every angle. Sometimes, to make you try on something horrible that she has just spotted on the bargain rail, she might even make you take your clothes off in the middle of the store with hundreds of strangers watching. These strangers might even point at your little soldier. This near-naked behaviour must be prevented at all times! It is not cool to be your mother's dolly. Girls *always* avoid a mummy's boy.

If your mother starts treating you like a dolly, you must waste no time in getting rid of her. Not with a hit man, obviously. Just tell her you've seen a lovely mummy dress in the ladies' department that would look beautiful on her, or pretend to sniff a delicious chocolate drink from the cafeteria. If this doesn't get rid of her, nothing will.

Learn this equation!

Chocolate + Mummy = Busy Maternal Gob
= End to Shop-a-Nightmare

The Changing Room Close-Up: If she refuses to leave you alone, don't let her stand outside the changing room where she has room to weave her embarrassing magic. Choose the clothes that you think are cool, then insist that she comes into the changing room with you, where the lack of space will ensure that you have the upper hand:

1. You are both hidden from view. If any of your friends happen to be in the store with *their* mums, they won't see you.

2. Due to the confines of the space she will be unable to step back far enough to take a proper look at you in your cool gear. In this way she won't see the full horror of what you've chosen till you get home!

3. Wear cheesy socks. She will be forced to smell them at close quarters and will want to get out of the changing room as quickly as possible. It goes without saying that the less time she spends inspecting your new clothes the more you can get away with.

The Easy-Listening Musak Sting: Ask for the in-store music to be turned UP. The louder the music the less you will hear what she's saying. Any objections she might have to your choice of cool clothes will therefore fall on deaf ears.

The Checkout Flimflam: When it comes to payment at the till, always pretend you've got a stomach-ache. This will make your mother anxious, and ensure that her attention is fixed on you when her credit card is swiped and *not* your new clothes, which she detests and told you she would not pay for!

WARNING: *Whether you are a boy who buys his own clothes or a boy who has his clothes bought for him, there is one gruesome aspect of shopping that people rarely discuss but that you should know about:* **SHOP ASSISTANTS IN TRENDY SHOPS ARE ONLY THERE TO MAKE YOU FEEL STUPID!** *It is their job to treat you as if you're less important than a boiled whelk. They will ignore you. They will not talk to you. They will sneer at you. And they will only take your money if you force it into their hands. You will mainly find these zombies in clothes or record shops, lurking behind pillars avoiding sales. Do not approach these ghouls, for they are the undead of cool! These people are terrifying examples of what can happen when being cool is taken too far. Beware their half-closed eyes and snarling lips. Attempt no communication. And do not smile. For in their mysterious other world a smile is "really sad, man" and they will snigger at you behind your back.*

TAKE A BREATHER...

Congratulations, you are one step closer to your first tongue sandwich! You have just completed the first eight steps in your quest to become a master of cool. You not only smell good and look good, but you dress good too. Very soon you will be ready to go out in public without wearing a paper bag or a pantomime horse. Before you can do this, however, you must first attain mastery of Step Nine.

Step Nine

Sound Cool

You can LOOK as cool as a Navajo's knapsack, but if all you SAY is grunt, gibe or garbage, you can forget about pulling. Girls want a boy who is loose-tongued and learned. Words are the thing. The right words in the right order. Here's how.

There are two types of cool-speak. One you speak in front of adults; the other you speak in front of girls.

Adult-Speak

It is a well-known fact that if you are understood by older people you are NOT cool. It is your duty as a would-be coolee to talk in tongues and confuse your parents. Make words up. If you've got friends round, gather them together in the sitting room and laugh at nonsense to make your parents feel stupid.

Here are a few words that were made up earlier to get you started:

shank . . . . boy

fidge . . . . an ugly spot on the end of a nose

shimble . . . . to be too shy to talk to a girl

shimbleshank . . . . a boy who is too shy to talk to a girl

fidgeshimbleshank . . . . a boy who is too shy to talk to a girl because of an ugly spot on the end of his nose

him . . . . a girl

chap . . . . a girl's giggly friend

hot lips . . . . ice cream

chapped lips . . . . sore lips after eating ice cream with a girl's giggly friend

Pinkerton's aeroplane? . . Shall we rush them now and push them out of that window?

Ouch! . . . . I like that!

Ouch! That really hurt! . . I like that a lot!

Aaaaaaggggghhhhhh! . . More please!

Now stickaminch some of your own pollyworms.

Girl-Speak

Of course, talking nonsense to a girl would be date-suicide. Remember, to think cool you must think older (see Step Three: **Think Cool**). She would soon get tired of your infantile gibberish and leave you for someone with basic conversational skills. Girls like boys who communicate.

Getting the Knowledge

Unfortunately for boys, girls are impressed by knowledge. This means that to be cool with girls, boys have got to know their stuff. They must be, or at least appear to be, intellectual.[4]

Becoming a real intellectual with letters after your name takes years of brown-nosing at cocktail parties, but you can sound intellectual in a matter of hours if you follow these six steps:

1. Read a WHOLE newspaper, not just the sports pages.
2. Watch all the news on TV, not just the sports reports.
3. Read books, encyclopedias and advertising posters. During mealtimes, read the backs

4 If you don't know what "intellectual" means, skip this section.

of cans. No matter how insignificant the information appears to be, read it. You never know what a girl might be into. She might be a canaholic, with plans to open her own canning factory when she grows up, or she might just have a thing about E-numbers.

4 Everyone loves films. To be cool you must always have an opinion about every film ever made in the world. Generally people think you're clever if you say a film is rubbish. So go and see every new film before your friends, then rush to school the next day and tell them what a load of pants it was! Unless it had a long car chase in it, lots of explosions and a couple of decapitations ... then it was brilliant. Films can easily be categorized according to content:

brilliant film = *guns, muscles, cars, kissing, graveyards*

rubbish film = *camels, costumes, dying, crying, horses*

5 Music is a vital topic of discussion to master if you are planning to pull at the school disco (see Phase Five: **Tackling Tongue Sushi**). Every girl will expect you to know about music. And not just boy-music like rap and garage; girl-music too, like boy bands and pop idols and big-nosed American singers who scare birds with songs about sinking boats. In case a girl ever asks you the killer question "What music are you into?" learn and

regurgitate the following answer as it generally shuts them up: *"I'm a technophonic stringless puppet, man, a wham-bam-thank-you-ham-jam kind of a guy, a dizzy disciple of the phonic fusion scene – heavy pop, classical bluegrass hip hop sort of sound, with a radical bass, indie garage groove inspired by MOBO, smoky jazz and Glam Shady's folk night in Motown. Not to mention Mersey Beat old-time rock 'n' roll crooners with a taste for solid music-hall gangsta rap and soul diva punk glamour flip-flop-in-the-house-flapperjack ... if you know what I mean?"*

6 Never, NEVER talk in a posh upper-class English accent. A Mancunian, Liverpudlian or Glaswegian accent is best as it tells girls that you are a working-class hero. If you sound like you come from Eton they will think you are an upper-class twit. If girls think your life has been one long struggle from teat to street, you are automatically cool!

Listening

A good conversation is as much about listening as it is about talking. And listening is much underrated as a snogging tool. Girls really love it when a boy listens to what they're saying.

So, use your mirror to practise intellectual listening looks. Aim to master the following facial expressions, as they will make girls love you more.

I'm listening to every word you are saying.

No, go on, I'm fascinated.

I care deeply about whatever it is you're droning on about.

I am nodding with real concern.

No, go on, I'm fascinated.

You want to talk about me and my life? Oh no, I'm boring. Let's talk about *you* some more.

I hate football.

Ballet and dressage! How did you know that they were my favourite sports?

No, go on, I'm fascinated.

OK.
YOU'RE READY...

PHASE THREE

TAKING YOUR FIRST COOL STEPS INTO THE BIG BAD WORLD

Step Ten

Look Good in the Hood

It is one thing to look and sound cool in the non-hostile environment of your bedroom. It is quite another to parade your cool on the streets where other boy cools are strutting their stuff, and jealousy can lead to cool hot spots where tempers fly and cools can be lost for ever. There are certain rules of cool that apply on the street. If you break these rules you will stop looking cool and start looking pants. So learn them.

Rule 1 WALK THE WALK

Do not apologize for yourself. Do not walk like you are scared of everyone around you. Give off a whiff of danger. Let passers-by know that the king of cool is in their midst and they'd better get down on their knees or out of your way! There are two types of walk that have cool approval from the Ministry of Surly Walks:

The Swagger: Here the shoulders are pushed back and the head is thrust forward. Bob down the street like there's music in your soul. Look everyone in the eye and don't be the first to look away. Don't give way for nobody, except possibly a policeman or a fit-looking girl. You are the prince of the pavement, the khan of the kerbstone, the grand duke of the gutter, and everyone else must give you respect!

The Slouch: Here the shoulders are rolled forward, the hands are thrust deep into the pockets, the head is bowed and the feet shuffle forward like a hobbled donkey. This Neanderthal troll look screams "unwashed animal" to the world. It says, "I am a caveman who won't be chained by your rules, and until you change them I'm going to sulk!"

"WELL, I NEVER KNEW THAT!"

FACT FILE #4

Sulking is an excellent weapon in the cool dude's armoury. Use it extensively to wear down your parents when they refuse to give you what you want. No matter how unreasonable your demands, you will always win. You are younger; your parents are older. They have less of their lives left to live, so they're in more of a hurry to get things done than you and will always give in first, saying stupid stuff like "If I were twenty years younger I wouldn't be giving in like this, you know!"

Chewing makes you look as though you're deep in thought even when you're not. Girls like deep thinkers. So, it doesn't matter what you put in your mouth, just make sure you're always chewing. Gum, cocktail stick, pen top, tree bark, bus ticket, shoelace, watch strap, fingernail, shirtsleeve, tongue, school tie or earwax.

Rule 3 PASS THE GLASS

Appearance is everything. You've just spent six months reading this book and learning how to look cool; you don't want all that work blown away by a puff of wind. It is therefore essential that you check your appearance every three seconds while out on the street. God forbid that your jeans might have ridden up and be covering your underpants! The best way to check yourself out is in shop windows, but you must NEVER be seen doing it! It is UNCOOL to care about your appearance in public. After all, the whole point of street cool is to make you look like a REBEL! If you don't look rough, like an unloved scarecrow – if your clothes don't look like they've been chucked on in the dark or your spiked hair doesn't look like you've just crawled out of a pit – the style statement isn't working! So by all means glance in the shop window, but don't let anyone catch you doing it.

Rule 4 HEAT THE SEAT

If you've got nothing to do, find somewhere to sit. A park bench, the stone plinth of a statue and a bus shelter are obvious places. A person sitting down looks like they've just come from somewhere and are about to go somewhere else. In other words, that person looks busy. And nobody notices a busy person. Therefore sitting down is a great way to stare at girls. This is why sitting on a bench is often referred to as sitting in the meat locker.

WARNING: *Never look bored when you're sitting down or people will assume you are a layabout and well-meaning women will try to delouse you. Keep your mind alert by playing games of Hunt the Hottie in your head.*

THE ANCIENT MIND GAME OF HUNT THE HOTTIE

This is a simple fantasy game for one player. It's a bit like Dungeons and Dragons only without the dungeons and without the dragons. You are walking through a beautiful garden full of lovely girls hiding behind every rock. Every girl loves you. All you have to do is find one and smile at her, and she will tell you what she finds attractive about you before she chews your face!

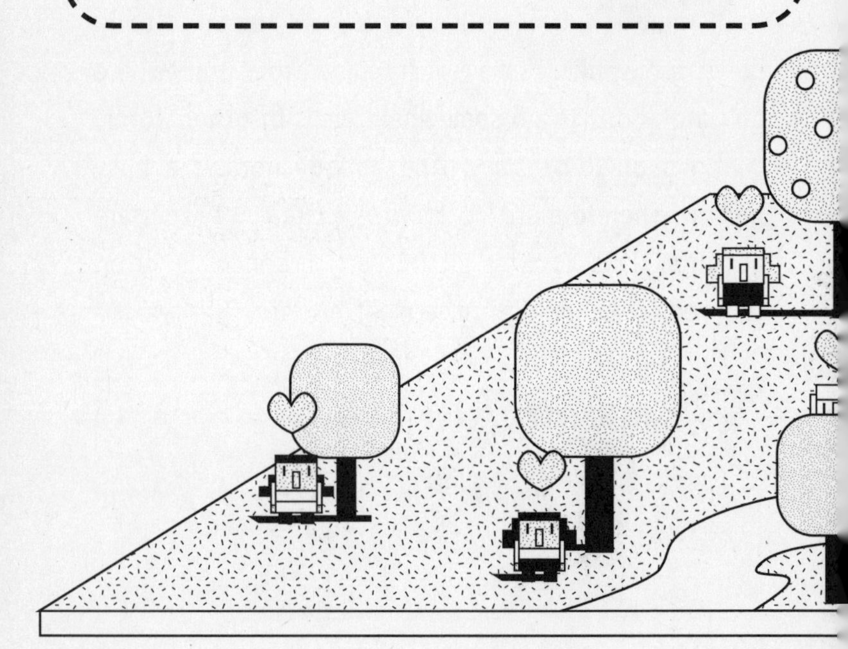

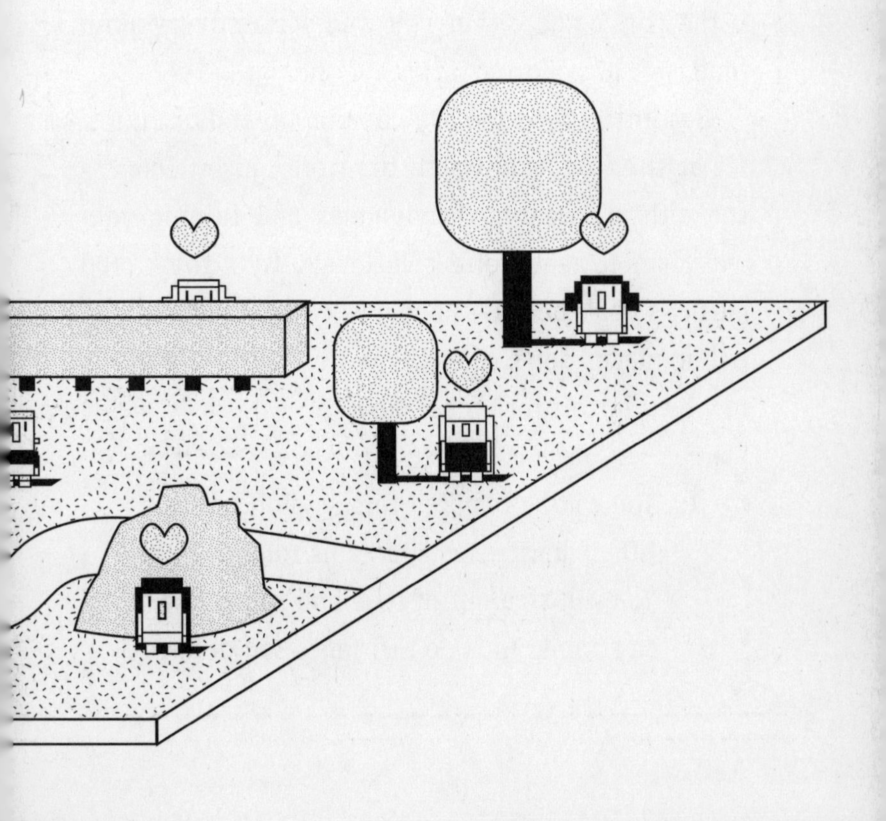

If it's raining, sitting outside is obviously stupid. Being cool is one thing; being freezing cold and soaking wet is quite another. Retiring into shopping centres is one option, but there's always the danger you might run into your mother, who will have a blue fit when she sees what you look like and will drag you off to shop for "nicer" or more "sensible" clothes – the sort of gear that you would classify as moth food.

Better to spend the day hopping on and off buses. Sit at the front and watch the world go by. Impress the girls by wearing headphones and turning your music up to really offensive levels. Girls think loud music is cool, because people who play loud music in public places don't care. There are, however, dangers involved in this rock rebel ploy:

1 You will be tempted to sing along. Under NO circumstances allow this to happen. You will sing out of tune and sound like a sad drunk. Girls do NOT fancy sad drunks.

2 Be careful when you step down off the bus. The loud music will have rendered you deaf and you will not hear the passing traffic. A car does not care if you are cool or not. It will squash you just the same.

Rule 6 VET THE PET

For total peace of mind, the rule of cool is to AVOID pets at all times. They are NOT cool.

1 It is a well-known fact that pets resemble their owners. For this reason a boy must never take an ugly, smelly pet out onto the street or girls will assume that he is ugly and smelly too.

2 Boys and girls like different pets. So what is sauce for the goose is not necessarily sauce for the gander.

PETS BOYS LIKE

bulldog

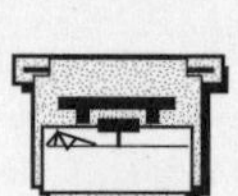
pit bull terrier

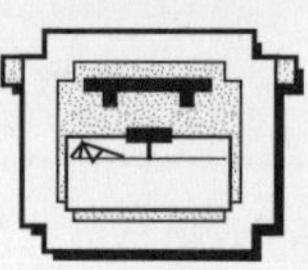
lion

Komodo dragon

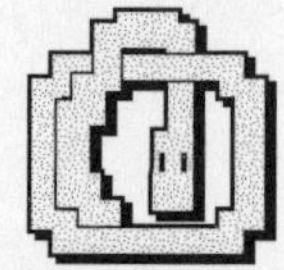
boa constrictor

ferret

bird-eating spider

spitting cobra

PETS GIRLS LIKE

fluffy rabbit

kitten

puppy

hamster

gerbil

mink

fox fur

chinchilla

These lists prove conclusively that if boys buy boys' pets for the sole purpose of attracting girls, they will not succeed, because girls do not like boys' pets. Unfortunately, if boys buy girls' pets to attract girls, they will not succeed either. If a girl sees a boy skipping down the street with a fluffy white rabbit on a lead, she will automatically dismiss him as an uncool sissy.

3 Pets are too unpredictable to be cool. For example, if you were talking to a girl by a bus stop and your dog did one of the following –

- peed on her shoes
- pooed in her rucksack
- cuddled her ankle with a grip of iron
- put his head up her skirt
- farted stink clouds up her nose

– the chances are she would never want to see you again!

Everyone needs wheels, but which set of wheels is the coolest? The following in-depth survey investigates the sex appeal of street transport:

Skateboard: A piece of chipped plywood and four castors off an old sofa – I'm sorry, but what is cool about that? Jumping twelve centimetres off the ground, using your own leg for propulsion, falling over kerbstones... It's not happening, is it? Not only that but you've got to wear protective pads, and wearing protective pads makes you look like a beginner. Girls like champions.

Monocycle: Cool for clowns. Are you a clown? Didn't think so.

Blades: Good for hanging onto buses and hitching free rides. Might make you look like a cheapskate who can't pay his own way, though. Beware.

Scooter: Cool until newborn babies start riding them. When that day comes, shoota dat scooter!

Bicycle: Do not be fooled into thinking that Lycra cycling shorts and T-shirts are sexy. Girls do not want to go to the cinema with a boy dressed in puke-coloured cling film.

Basic bikes get you from A to B, but they are boring. A bit like a banana fills you up, but where's the thrill? Add ice cream, nuts, chocolate sauce, raspberry jam, hundreds and thousands, and lashings of whipped cream, and you create a super banana!

If you want a banana split of a bike that will make you stand out from the crowd and mark you out as the coolest rider on the block, you need ALL of the extras...

1 *chrome spokes*
2 *quick release wheel nuts*
3 *front suspension forks*
4 *rude stickers*
5 *front indicators (right and left)*
6 *front musical brake pads*
7 *air bag*
8 *halogen front lamp*
9 *furry dice*
10 *wing mirrors (right and left)*
11 *bell*
12 *klaxon*
13 *whistle rest*
14 *notebook and pen holder for recording car number plates*
15 *CD player and radio*
16 *mobile phone holder*
17 *mobile phone amplifier*
18 *mobile phone microphone*
19 *indicator switch*
20 *gear shift*
21 *pump*
22 *speedometer*
23 *milometer*
24 *go-faster stripe*
25 *more rude stickers*
26 *water bottle holder*
27 *emergency tool kit*
28 *emergency torch*
29 *emergency triangle for breakdown abroad*
30 *emergency Lycra leotard*
31 *emergency food rations*
32 *emergency butane gas cooker*
33 *emergency tent*
34 *tungsten steel padlock*
35 *carbon fibre pedals (right and left)*
36 *Day-Glo pedal reflector strips (right and left)*
37 *extendable saddle suspension system*
38 *gel saddle*
39 *gel saddle cushioned cover*
40 *gel saddle cushioned cover cover*
41 *rear halogen lamp*
42 *rear suspension forks*
43 *rear indicators (right and left)*
44 *rear musical brake pads*
45 *even more rude stickers*
46 *rucksack rack*
47 *surround-sound speakers*
48 *525-litre "Tardis" saddlebags*
49 *36 synchromesh gears*

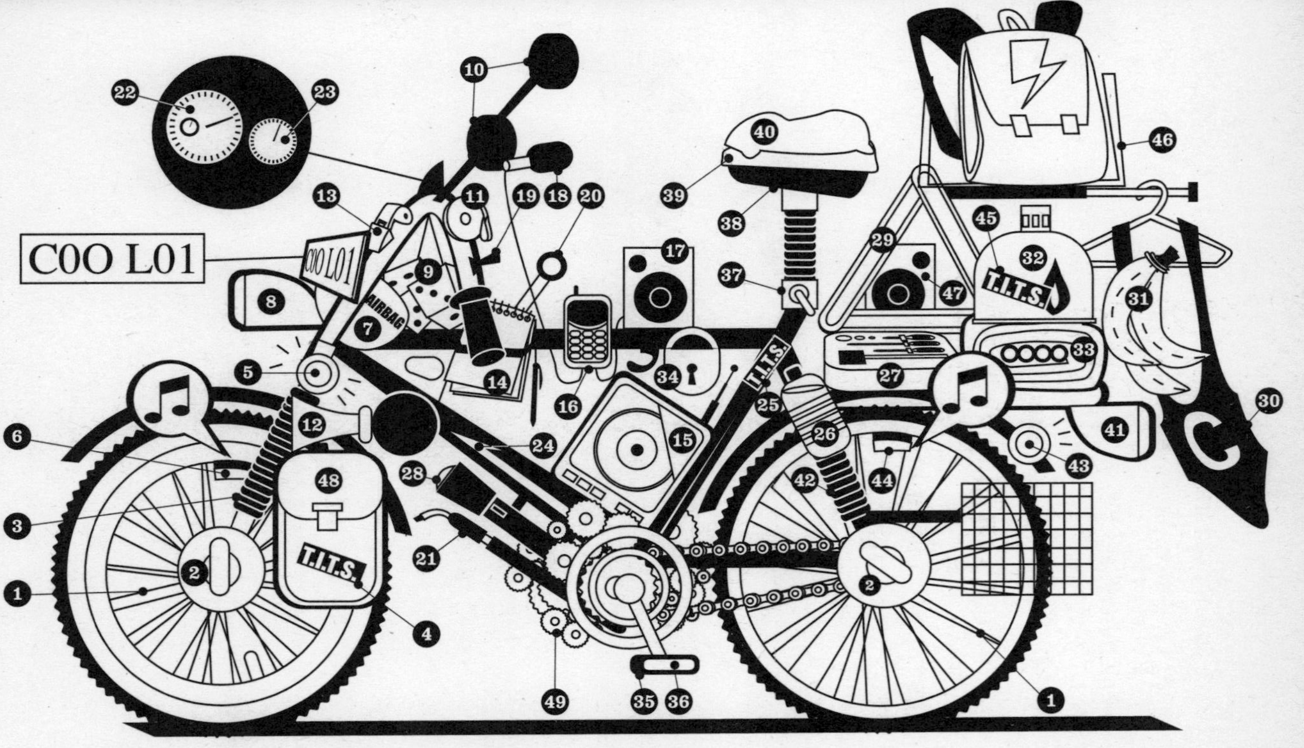

This is a cool bike. Unfortunately it weighs six and a half tons and can only be moved if towed by a tractor.

Now that you have learned how to walk, talk and look cool both indoors and out, it is time to remember WHY you wanted to become cool in the first place. Remember?

Q: But will I get snogged?
A: Yes. That's the whole idea, isn't it?

It's time to pucker up and ring that bell! Next stop – Kiss City Central!

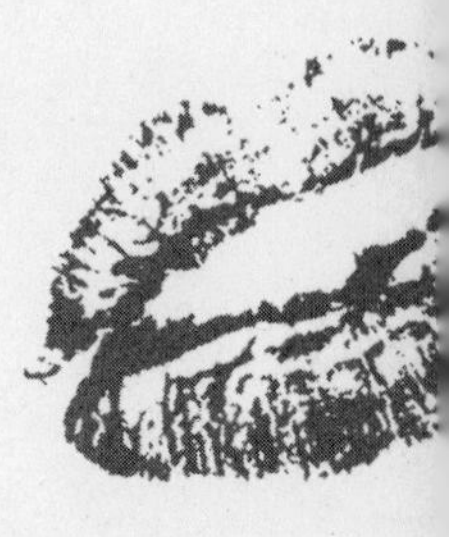

PHASE FOUR

GETTING BUSY WITH LIZZIE

Step Eleven

Using Cool to Get Yourself Noticed

Now that you have mastered the appearance of cool, it's time to put your new-found talents to the test. Girls occupy half of the planet and can be found almost everywhere. So if you want to get yourself noticed by girls you should have your cool prepared at all times.

At School: You will meet most girls at school. Therefore you must always be alert to the possibility that the girl of your dreams is sitting at the next table drinking Um Bongo. For this reason alone, you must never be off-cool at school.

The coolest way to catch a girl's attention is to be different. Don't swim with the shoal. Be eccentric, because when you stand out you get noticed.

1. Take a mid-morning nap in the classroom.
2. Use the girls' loos and smile when they scream.
3. Do your homework, but hand it in to the wrong teacher.
4. Change your name to Hercules Hairy Loveboat and insist that the teacher alters the register.
5. Eat green vegetables in the playground at break. "Mmm, broccoli-flavoured crisps again. Anyone fancy a nibble?"
6. Arrive at school in a pedal car.
7. Wear a Stetson and a sheriff's badge for swimming club.

On the Sports Field: Girls are not overly keen on boys who spend ALL their time watching and playing sport. Sport eats into chatting time, which is what girls prefer to do. On the other hand, sport is the modern-day equivalent of war, in which team is pitted against team like armies of yore, and history proves that girls have always been partial to a bit of blood and gore in the gladiatorial arena or jousting park so long as the combatants are fighting over them!

SPORTS THAT GIRLS APPROVE OF

- ☑ tiddlywinks
- ☑ netball
- ☑ curling
- ☑ dressage
- ☑ ribbon gymnastics
- ☑ synchronized swimming
- ☑ short tennis
- ☑ competitive basket weaving
- ☑ gardening

SPORTS THAT GIRLS DO NOT APPROVE OF

- ☒ pulling lorries
- ☒ football
- ☒ basketball
- ☒ jet fighter acrobatics
- ☒ go-karting
- ☒ rowing
- ☒ Xtreme tennis
- ☒ sumo wrestling
- ☒ rock somersaulting

Nowadays, however, girls prefer to watch the likes of Russell Crowe and Bruce Willis hacking lumps off each other. They do not want to see their boyfriend lose a limb. One can say with some certainty that if a modern boy was to lose a leg in modern gladiatorial combat, a modern girl would not stand by him. Which would be a shame, because without her support and with only one leg, modern boy would keep falling over.

Having said this, a moderate interest in sport is cool. It displays manliness and bravery, which most girls still find attractive. Therefore boys should find a sport that girls approve of and play it occasionally.

On the Stage: Girls love the theatre. They enjoy acting and showing off to their friends. Boys tend to be more embarrassed about standing on a stage in tights. But as somewhere to meet girls, rehearsals for the school play are second to none. Boys – you will be outnumbered twenty to one. Make the girls LAUGH by making a fool of yourself in front of them and they will all want to meet you. You will be wallowing in girl-clover!

SEVENTH RULE OF COOL:
Play the fool

Q: How do I make a fool of myself?

A: Volunteer for anything and everything. Sooner or later you are bound to find something you are bad at, and bad equals funny. Wear silly costumes, dress up in animal suits, pretend to be a girl.[5] Abandon self-consciousness. Do whatever it takes to turn yourself into a figure of fun, and if that means resorting to the comic feather duster – wave it with conviction! If you still need convincing, it has been scientifically proven that even ugly boys can attract girls by being funny!

At the Bus Stop: Waiting for a bus after school is a good place to impress girls with your new-found cool. Slouch against a wall or lamppost, chew gum and ignore them. You will probably notice the girls doing exactly the same thing. This means that they find you attractive.

Move on to the next step. 

5 There is one female role that no boy should take, no matter how much he wants to impress the girls. Kate in *Kiss Me, Kate*. The role involves at least sixty-three snogs with testosterone-fuelled boys. Nuff said.

Step Twelve

How Do I Know Which Girl to Fancy?

Your eccentric behaviour at school, on the playing fields and on the stage will have got you noticed. You are cool because you are unique. There's nobody quite like you. But you still haven't TALKED to a girl, let alone asked one out. We all know that it is nearly impossible for a boy to open his mouth and talk to a girl for the first time.[6] But we also know that if you *don't* speak to a girl it is impossible to have any sort of relationship with her beyond longing looks and hair-tossing.

6 If it's any consolation, speaking to the opposite sex for the first time is no easier for girls. They are just as nervous as you are and although they might appear to be aloof goddesses, their feet are made of clay just like yours.

So how do you turn first contact into something altogether more meaningful? How do you push on into a one-to-one situation? How do you know which girl you fancy?

Choosing the Lucky Girl!

This is easier said than done. How do you decide which girl is the one you want to pull out of all the lovely girls available? It's like being in a restaurant and wanting EVERYTHING on the menu!

Here's how you know. Look deep into a girl's eyes. Girls to whom you are NOT physically attracted will make you feel sick. Girls to whom you ARE physically attracted will give you butterflies in the pit of your stomach. QED!

Q: But butterflies in the pit of your stomach feel just like an upset tummy, and an upset tummy makes you feel sick. So if not liking a girl and liking a girl both make you feel the same, how can you tell which one it is you are feeling?

A: Good question. That would explain why I always end up dancing with girls I don't like.

Q: Shall I forget the stomach advice then?

A: I would if I were you. Ask me again.

Q: So how will I know when I fancy a girl?

A: Simple. When your eyes shoot halfway across the room, when your heart pounds against your ribs like a kangaroo trapped in a greenhouse, when your knees wobble faster than a jelly baby in a tumble-dryer and when your mouth is too dry to speak.

Q: Thank you. Can't wait.

Q: Hang on. If my mouth is too dry to speak, how do I ask her out?

A: Next step.

Step Thirteen

How to Ask Her Out Without Losing Cool

Your mouth will not stay dry for ever. If it does you have been buried alive and should immediately seek the assistance of a gravedigger. When you regain your voice it will be time to speak, and when you do it is imperative that what you say is cool.

Q: Now you're making me nervous again. What do I say?

A: Where do you want to take her on your first date?

Q: How about the school disco?

A: OK. There are many ways to ask a girl out, and here are a few of the bad ones...

Uncool Ways to Ask a Girl Out

It is often more useful to know what NOT to do in certain circumstances, as this ensures that you do things properly:

1 **DON'T** slip a love poem into her rucksack.

Roses are red,
Violets are blue,
Only the prettiest flowers
Remind me of you.

She will show it to all of her friends and you will be mocked for the rest of your life. Girls have memories like elephants. Occasionally they may forgive, but they NEVER forget.

2 **DON'T** send her a text message saying **Xcus me can u giv me drctns 2 ya <3?** She will reply **Gt lst** and change her mobile phone number.

3 **DON'T** approach her in the playground and say, "Your father must be a thief, because he stole the stars out of the sky and put them in your eyes." She will be sick. There is also a chance that if her father is a thief she will punch you in the head.

4 **DON'T** say, "Hello. You're pretty. Did you make that beautiful top yourself?" You will sound like her grandmother.

5 **DON'T** bump into her and say, "Whoops! Sorry. Your dazzling smile blinded me for a moment and I couldn't see where I was going." You will probably break her collarbone by accident.

6 And under **NO** circumstances produce a Barbie doll from your pocket and say, "Her air stewardess uniform is my favourite. Want to play?" She will think you are a freaky creature from the planet Lesbos, where all men are really women.

Cool Ways to Ask a Girl Out

"Would you like to go to the school disco with me?"

RESULT!

So you've asked her out and she's said yes. Now you need to prepare for the big day and that first kiss.

PHASE FIVE

TACKLING TONGUE SUSHI

Step Fourteen

You've Got a Tongue in Your Head – Use It!

It is a common error for newly cool boys to wake up on the morning of the biggest day of their lives (in other words, kiss minus twelve hours and counting!) only to discover that they don't know how to do it. So my best advice is, if you want to remain cool, check that you know how to kiss WELL IN ADVANCE of the disco. Where kissing is concerned, ignorance is NOT bliss. Quite the opposite in fact. There is nothing more repulsive for a girl than a mouthful of dead tongue. It's like having sloppy frogs in her mouth.

Myths

There are a few myths about kissing that must be dispelled:

1. It does not give you dog breath.
2. It is extremely hard to bite someone's tongue off unless you really try.
3. Two tongues are company but three are a crowd.
4. Thirty tongues DO make a snogathon.
5. You cannot catch stupidity from kissing a fool.
6. Footballers are not all gay.

The golden rule is this: if you are in any doubt about what to do, ASK! You've got a tongue in your head, so use it.

Q: How useful are big sisters?

A: Not very, to be honest. Big sisters tend to be a waste of a good skin. They're much more interested in themselves than in you. But they do have one useful function.

Q: Which is?

A: Kissing lessons.

Q: Kissing lessons ... with your sister!

A: No. Wait! Stop! You've got the wrong end of the stick. Come back!

Under no circumstances kiss your own sister. This will result in both of you growing tusks. Pump your big sister for INFORMATION ONLY on kissing. Questions like:

1. What is the best angle to approach a girl's lips? From above, below, straight on or behind?
2. Do girls like having raspberries blown on their lips during a kiss?
3. Can you name one thing that is pleasant about running your tongue along someone else's teeth?
4. What if she's eaten fish paste and I can taste it? I hate fish paste.
5. Is holding hands too forward on a first kiss?

6 Should I keep the conversation flowing DURING the kiss?

7 What happens if her brace interlocks with mine and we are still stuck together eight hours later? Will we have to get married?

8 Can I stop kissing to breathe or will she think I'm rude?

9 How do I finish a kiss when I've had enough? Would the raising of a flag be too impersonal?

These, and many more, are important questions that you must know the answer to before taking the plunge. There is nothing LESS cool than not knowing how to kiss a girl when you're trying to kiss a girl. If in doubt, ask your sister!

EIGHTH RULE OF COOL:
Know your BIG sister's onions

Step Fifteen

Last-Minute Preparations Before Your First Tongue Sushi

There is one hour to go before the school disco. Now it's time for some personal attention. Ooh la la!

The Warm-Up

Sit down in front of a mirror and ask yourself this. "Do I want to pull tonight?" If the answer is "Yes!" or even "Too lip-smacking right I do! I'm a bird-mad monster, me! My tongue is hanging out for a tonsil tickling!" you must do your tongue exercises. Remember, a strong tongue is a well-prepared tongue.

Open your mouth wide and stick your tongue out as far as it will go, then say *bleugh-leugh-leugh-leugh-leugh* as fast as you can for thirty seconds. Follow this with thirty seconds of *la-la-la-la-la* and thirty seconds of *mi-mi-mi-mi-mi*. Even if you don't pull tonight, you will always be able to sing at the Metropolitan Opera.

The Wash and Brush-Up

Wash. Brush teeth. Do not make the mistake of thinking that girls like unwashed boys. They do not. Imagine the poor girl's horror if she kisses your ear and sucks down a mouthful of cabbages!

"WELL, I NEVER KNEW THAT!"

FACT FILE #5

While in the bath always take precautions against unwanted visitors. A nosy sister or mother will often barge into the bathroom apparently looking for a hairbrush when really she's just trying to peek at the development of your little soldier. You are right to be embarrassed by this behaviour. It must be stopped. Here's how. Submerge a loofah in the bath, place a flannel over your little soldier, then close your eyes, lie back and wait for the intruder to sneak in. When you hear the door creak, position the loofah under the flannel and push up. If the peeping Tina hasn't screamed and rushed out of the bathroom within ten seconds she is almost certainly blind.

The Hip-Up

Most importantly, learn how to dance. Girls love dancing and no boy ever pulled by standing around the edge of the dance floor pretending to study curtain rings. If you are concerned that you can't dance or that, when you do, you look like an electrocuted heffalump, read and digest the following guide to cool dancing:

POCKET GUIDE TO COOL DANCING
This guide has been produced as a series of pocket-sized cards which you can cut out and keep handy. You may refer to the appropriate card in the event of a serious dancing emergency, such as knotted arms or feet.

Arms

- **DO NOT** put your hands in your pockets. You will look bored.
- **DO NOT** wave them wildly. You will only bash another girl in the mouth and knock out her teeth.
- If you knock out an innocent girl's teeth the disco will come to an abrupt end while she's whisked off to hospital. Plus, all the other girls will throw cheese and pineapple chunks at you for being such a clumsy lummox. Your chances of kissing a girl after bashing one of them in the mouth are not good. Your chances of kissing the Queen, her ladies-in-waiting, all her corgis and Lieutenant Uhura from *Star Trek* are better. So stay controlled.

Basic arm movements

• Pulling a pint

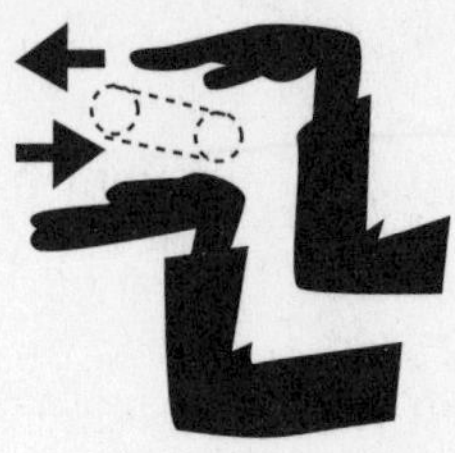

• Rolling a crispy duck pancake

• Hitch-hiking

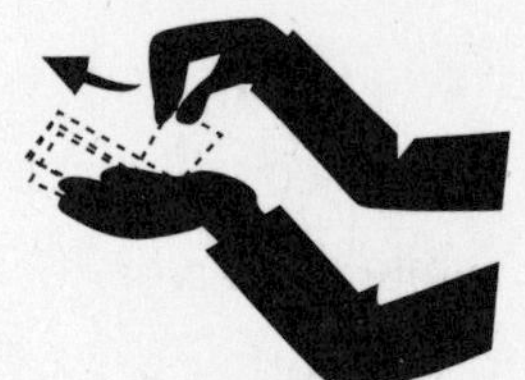

• Dealing cards

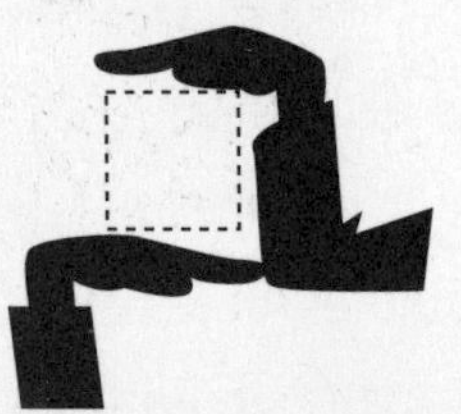

• Cardboard box

• Swan taking off

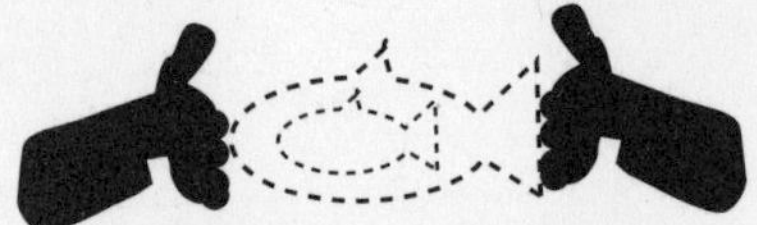

• Big fish, little fish

Legs

- **DO NOT** put your legs in your pockets either or you will need a hip replacement.
- Keep one foot on the ground at all times or you will quickly lose friends when you accidentally kick them up the bum and tread on their toes.
- **NO POGO.**

Basic leg movements Part I

The chicken walk

Raise right leg until knee is horizontal to hip. Lower right leg. Raise left leg until knee is horizontal to hip. Lower left leg.

Carry on chicken walking until (a) people exclaim how uncanny the resemblance is between you and an animal with a brain the size of a gnat's testicle and (b) you lay an egg.

Basic leg movements Part II

Rubber legs

Keep both feet firmly planted on ground. Then, like a windmill, rotate the knees in opposite directions at the same time.

Avoid clash of kneecaps or sparks will fly and trousers may catch fire.

Basic leg movements Part III

The moonwalk

If you can do the moonwalk you will be the coolest dude in the whole universe! Even Michael Jackson can't do it without help. Apparently, under his shoes he's got remote-controlled cars, which are operated from the side of the stage. It's true.

1

2

3

4

Basic leg movements Part IV

The spin

Only advanced dancers should try the spin. Failure to execute a full 360-degree spin can result in an ungainly tumble into the lap of the girl of your dreams. You will bundle her to the floor with her dress round her ears and she will never talk to you again. And quite right too! XXXtreme dancing, as the police call it, is banned everywhere in the world except Ireland.

4

Eyes open or closed?

- Definitely open. If you dance with your eyes closed she might slip away and you'd never know. You could end up dancing with a wall, or worse still a standard lamp, and not find out until it was too late.
- If your eyes are closed and you kiss a standard lamp by mistake you will never live it down. Especially if you cry out "Oh yeah, baby, you kiss good!" while everyone's watching.
- If you keep your eyes open be careful not to stare at her too intensely. She might start to think you're an axe murderer!

You are now a cool dancer with great breath and a loose tongue. Let the disco begin...

Step Sixteen

Check Your Ripcord

The disco has started. You are standing on the edge of the dance floor with the girl of your dreams. She is pretending not to have noticed that everyone else is dancing except you, but she has, and the DJ has just put on a slow, smoochy number. It's now or never.

The Pull

There is no going back now. Your transformation from ordinary Joe into boy cool will be complete when you kiss your first girl. The clock is ticking. Here is what you do:

1. **DON'T PANIC.**
2. **DON'T PANIC.**
3. **DON'T PANIC.**
4. **DON'T PANIC.** Your heart is meant to sound like a kettledrum thumping away inside your chest.
5. Drink a glass of water to wet your whistle.
6. Say something to her. Don't call her a bird. Don't ask her if she wants a long wet snog with breathing breaks. Don't ask her if she wants to taste the cheese and onion crisps you ate half an hour ago. Say what you mean. Be direct. "Would you like to dance?" Remember, GIRLS ARE PEOPLE TOO. They are not aliens from another planet. They have feelings just like

everyone else. She will dance if you ask her.

NINTH RULE OF COOL: Girls are humans too

7 Dance your way towards heaven! Once the two of you are dancing, you are but one short lunge away from your first kiss! Before you can lunge, however, you must first find out if she is available or whether she's attached to another. Disguise your cunning questions among a whole load of innocent ones. Like this:
"Oh, by the way [INSERT GIRL'S NAME], I forgot to ask. Do you live locally? Do you like ballet? Ever seen a cockroach the size of a mouse? Have you got a boyfriend? Has anyone ever told you that you look like my mum? What big feet you've got. Are those new socks you've got on? Do you like big pets? I do. I love heavy petting."

If she doesn't have a boyfriend and likes heavy petting you are looking good for a tongue sandwich. Now all you have to do is choose your moment.

8 The right moment to lean forward is not when you are doing a fast dance. When you dance fast your feet are all over the place and your balance is compromised. If you lean forward to kiss her when you're off balance, you will end up nutting her by mistake.

When you dance slow, however, your feet hardly move at all. You can lean forward without breaking her nose until you are face to face. Now brush your cheek against hers. Don't be shy. If you aren't brave enough to go the whole hog and make contact, pretend that someone just pushed you in the back, and lurch forward with a cry of "Oi! Watch it!" If she backs away, she doesn't want to kiss you. If she doesn't back away, BULLSEYE! You've got yourself a winner!

9 Go for the pull! Nobody can pull for you. You can't ask your mum and dad to help. This is something you have to do on your own. It's like jumping into a freezing cold swimming pool or eating a witchetty grub. You've just got to do it. Kiss her. Don't worry, she will let you know if she doesn't like it. With a slap probably, or a sharp knee in the groin!

CONGRATULATIONS!

YOU HAVE JUST KISSED A GIRL!

YOU ARE NOW

OFFICIALLY

COOL!

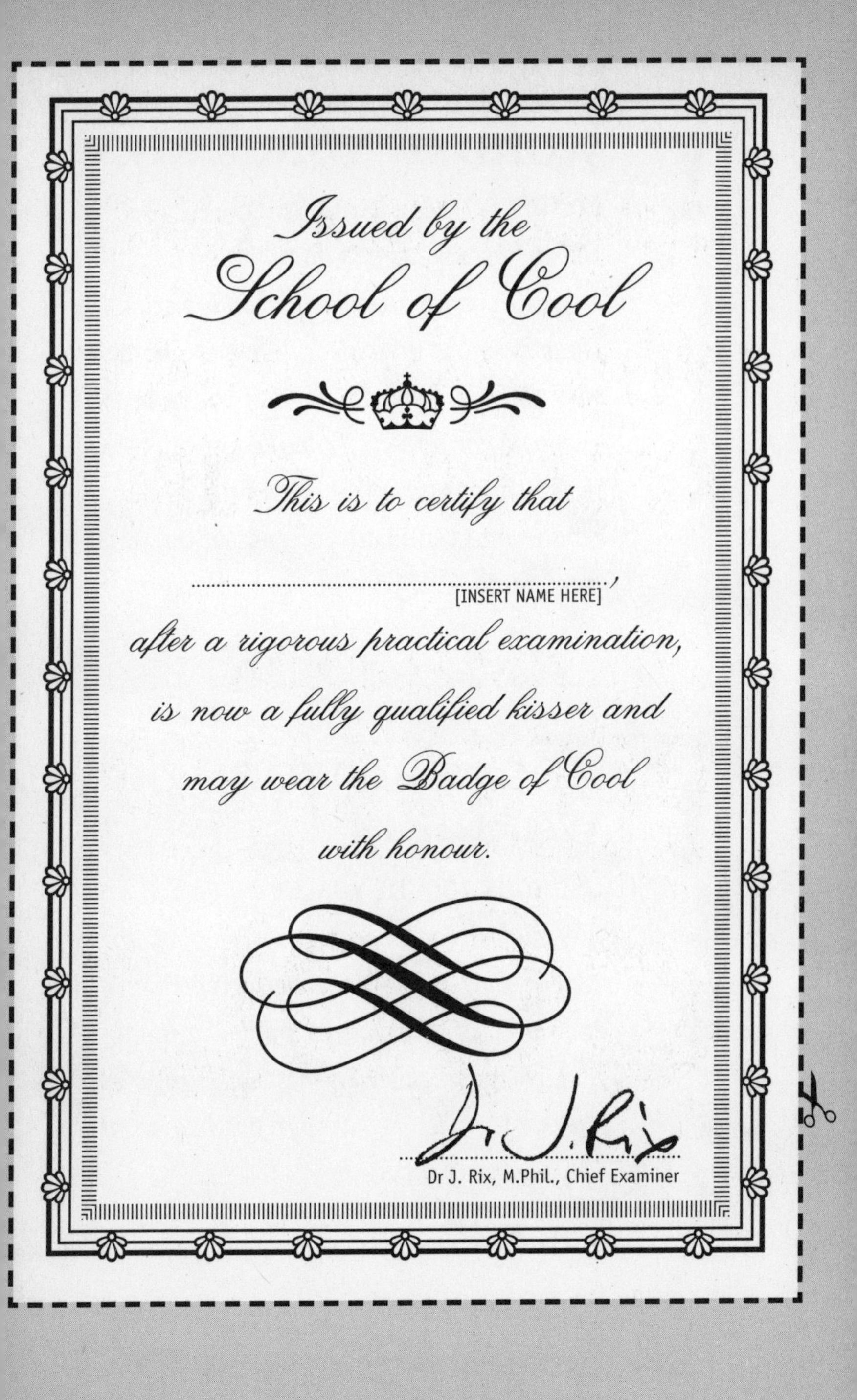
Issued by the
School of Cool
This is to certify that
....,
[INSERT NAME HERE]
after a rigorous practical examination,
is now a fully qualified kisser and
may wear the Badge of Cool
with honour.
Dr J. Rix, M.Phil., Chief Examiner

WORD OF WARNING!

DO NOT OUTSTAY YOUR WELCOME

The coolest kissers kiss all night, only occasionally coming up for air and biscuits. Three hours is normal, but five is impressive. You can generally judge if you've been snogging for an acceptable length of time if the tip of your nose is numb, you have ground one centimetre of enamel off your front teeth, and your lips are so sore that they split when you speak.

ANOTHER WORD OF WARNING!

USE YOUR TONGUE WISELY

Any sudden or unexpected thrust of the tongue may cause an adverse reaction in the throat of your partner similar to that of a retching seagull when its baby pecks at the spot on its beak. Your partner might very well park a custard.

TENTH RULE OF COOL:
Never let a girl park a custard on you

PHASE SIX

COOL FOR LIFE!

Step Sixteen and a Half

You Are Your Own Man Now

Now that you've had your first kiss you won't look back. Being cool is now in your soul and kissing girls will be as much a part of your everyday life as picking your teeth or dislodging a persistent lump of phlegm from your throat.

However, if as a result of the kiss you suddenly find yourself in a fully committed, long-term relationship which has lasted almost TWO weeks, you may be glad of the following advice...

1. If you take your girlfriend to the cinema, check the film's rating. There is nothing worse than buying tickets for an eighteen and asking for two halves.

2. If you *are* taking her to see a fifteen or an eighteen film, stick on a false moustache, wear high heels or stuff newspaper inside your shoes, and eat a large pot of yoghurt to thicken your voice and make you sound more manly.

3. She will want to go into a photo booth and take a series of embarrassing photographs. Do it or she'll leave you.

4. If you wish to take her out for a romantic dinner *à deux* on your first anniversary (first WEEK, that is), take her to a burger bar. Girls won't tell you this, but they love chips and chocolate more than boys.

5. When she phones you to ask you if you are missing her since she last phoned you, resist the temptation to shout, "Get a life! It was only two minutes ago!"

6. When she texts you eighty times a day to tell you how much she loves you, this is perfectly normal and *will* drive you round the twist. It is also perfectly normal to smash your mobile phone against the wall when the text tone interrupts your homework for the sixteenth time.

7. Do not let your parents produce the family photo albums when she's in the house. They will show her those pictures of you without any pants on, and that will be the end of boy cool for ever!

8 Do not let your father show her his tattoos. She will be scared.

9 Do not keep a diary of your love. Do not write her soppy poetry. Do not send her cards addressed to Cuddle-Dumpling and Squidgy. All of these will be found by your classmates and passed down the coach before swimming.

10 Never introduce your girlfriend to your brothers and sisters, because they will make a big joke out of it. They will tease you and say that as a baby she was beaten with the ugly stick.

11 When she gives you love bites on your neck, wear a scarf.

12 Never moisturize in front of your girlfriend or she will think you care more about yourself than you do about her.

13 Don't call her Mummy.

14 Never buy her a teddy bear. There will be custody problems when you split up.

15 When you do finally split up, you will be extremely upset if she dumps you first. You will feel like she has torn out your heart and beaten it with a sledgehammer. So make sure you dump her first! That is the cool way. Then she will feel really bad, not you.

16 If you dump her face to face she will cry. There are two courses of action:

A Buy her some sweets. Then she won't mind so much.

B Run away and pretend you don't know her.

17 Text messaging is an exciting new way to say goodbye with a blunt axe. Popular messages include **I am dead. Do not try 2 contact me** and **U r the wkst link. Gdbye.**

18 In fact, there are many, many ways to dump a girlfriend – phone, fax, letter, email, carrier pigeon and aeroplane towing banner in the sky – but the best and easiest way is to move house so she can never find you again.

THE TEN RULES OF COOL

FIRST RULE OF COOL:
There are no rules

SECOND RULE OF COOL:
Be yourself

THIRD RULE OF COOL:
Girls like boys who have more to say for themselves than "All right?" and "Smashing blouse you've got on!"

FOURTH RULE OF COOL:
Fart first, laugh later

FIFTH RULE OF COOL:
Don't be a sheep

SIXTH RULE OF COOL:
Cool at school means
break the rule

SEVENTH RULE OF COOL:
Play the fool

EIGHTH RULE OF COOL:
Know your BIG sister's
onions

NINTH RULE OF COOL:
Girls are humans too

TENTH RULE OF COOL:
Never let a girl park
a custard on you

EMERGENCY COOL KIT

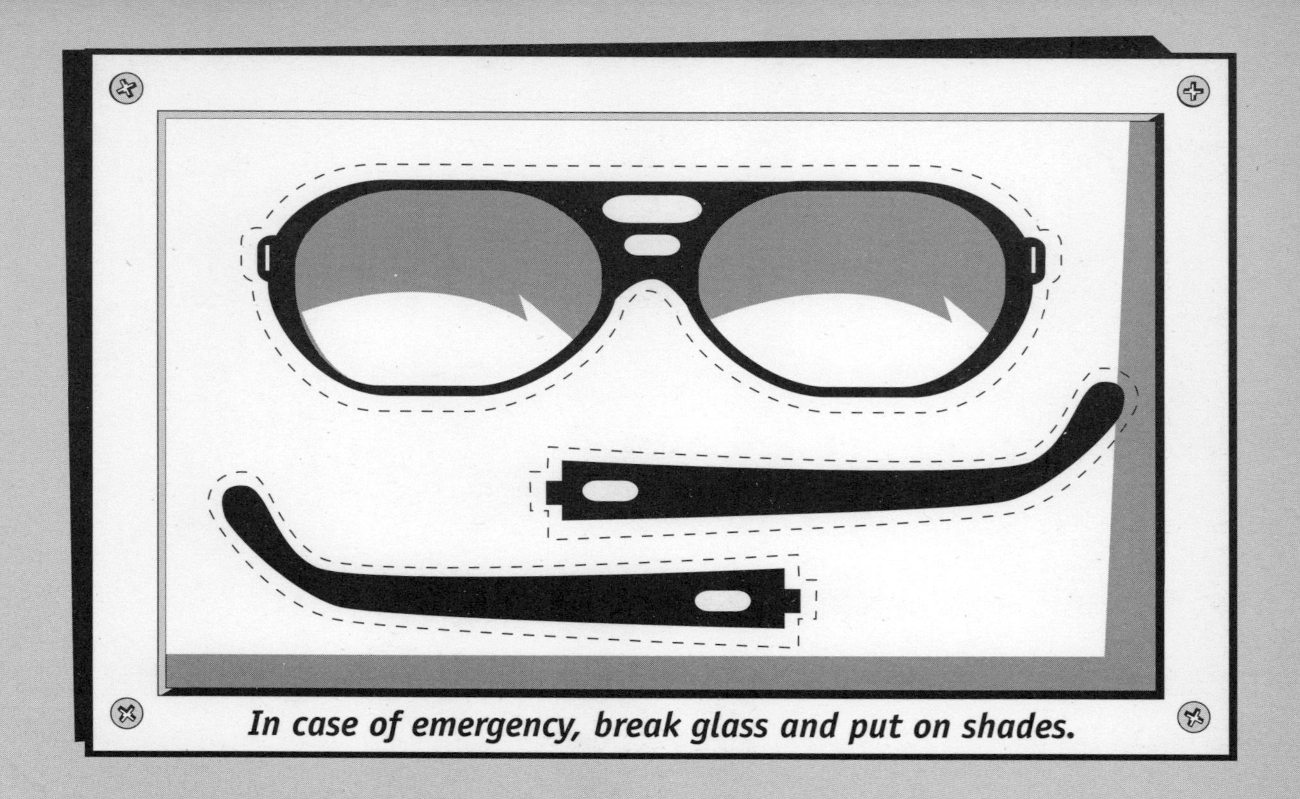
In case of emergency, break glass and put on shades.